THE STEM FILES

TOP SECRET: CHEMX

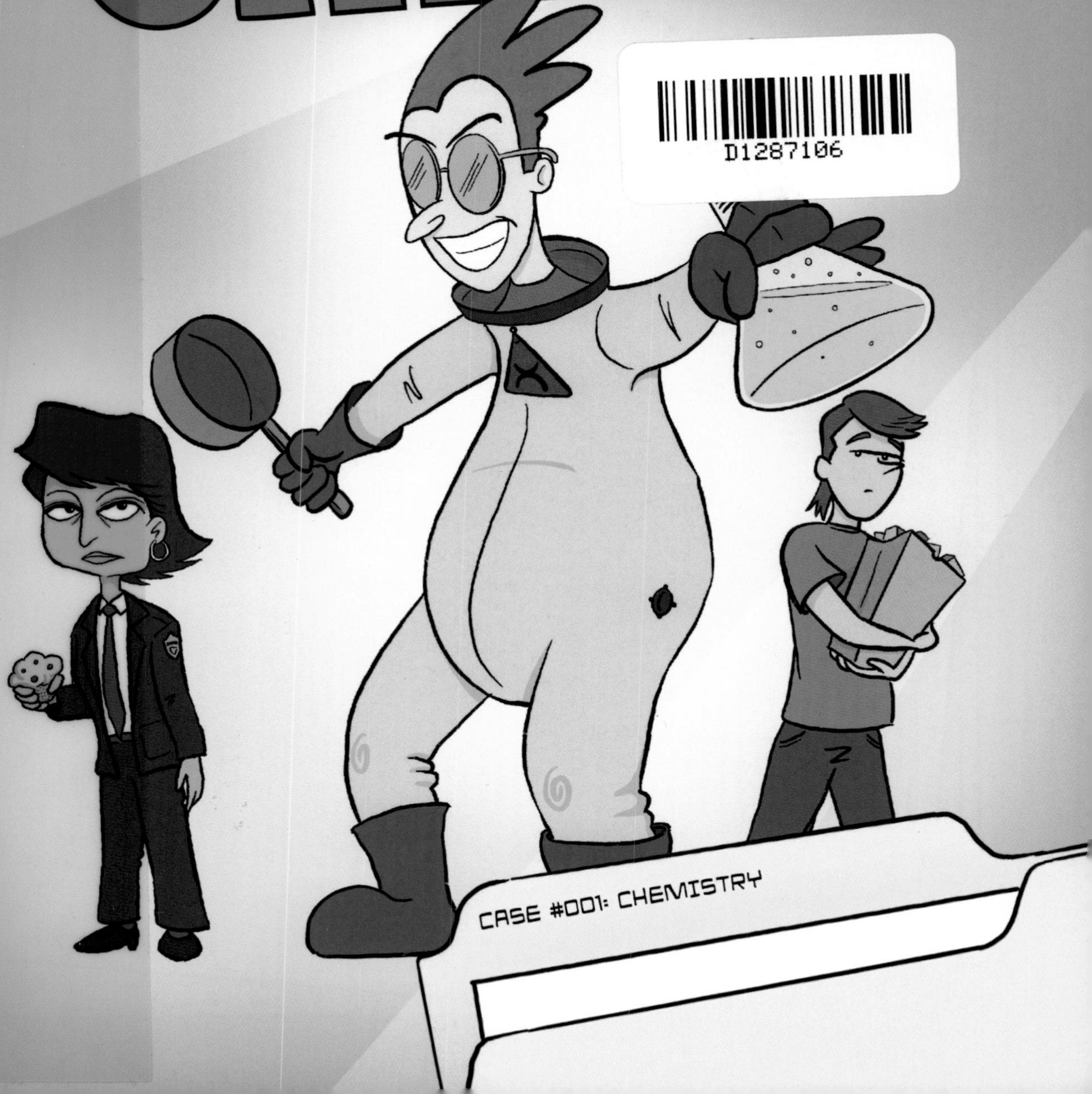
CASE #001: CHEMISTRY

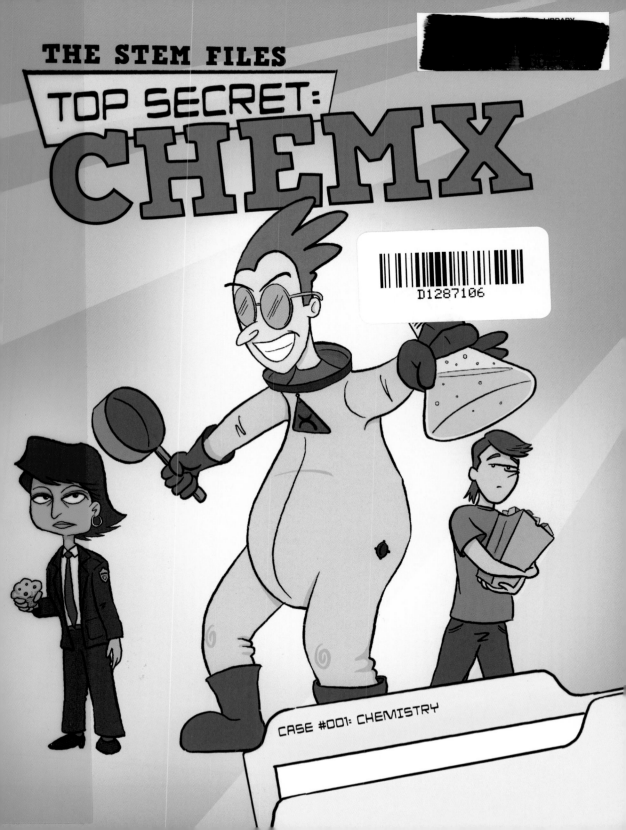

TORCH GRAPHIC PRESS

Published in the United States of America by Cherry Lake Publishing Group
Ann Arbor, Michigan
www.cherrylakepublishing.com

Story & Illustrator: D.C. London
Color & Character Design: John Boissy
Reading Adviser: Marla Conn, MS, Ed., Literacy specialist, Read-Ability, Inc.
Content Adviser: Stacy Chin, PhD
Production Artists: Jen Wahi, Mary Wagner, Jessica Rogner

Torch Graphic Press is an imprint of Cherry Lake Publishing Group.

Library of Congress Cataloging-in-Publication Data

Names: London, D. C., author.
Title: Top secret: ChemX / written by D.C. London.
Other titles: ChemX
Description: Ann Arbor, Michigan : Cherry Lake Publishing, [2020] | Series:
  The STEM files | Includes bibliographical references and index. |
Identifiers: LCCN 2020006975 (print) | LCCN 2020006976 (ebook) | ISBN
  9781534169357 (hardcover) | ISBN 9781534171039 (paperback) | ISBN
  9781534172876 (pdf) | ISBN 9781534174719 (ebook)
Subjects: LCSH: Graphic novels. | CYAC: Graphic novels. | Water
  supply--Fiction. | Chemistry--Fiction. | Villains--Fiction.
Classification: LCC PZ7.7.L663 Tog 2020 (print) | LCC PZ7.7.L663 (ebook)
  | DDC 741.5/973--dc23
LC record available at https://lccn.loc.gov/2020006975
LC ebook record available at https://lccn.loc.gov/2020006976

Cherry Lake Publishing Group would like to acknowledge the work of the
Partnership for 21st Century Learning, a Network of Battelle for Kids.
Please visit http://www.battelleforkids.org/networks/p21 for more information.

Printed in the United States of America
Corporate Graphics

About the Artist: D.C. London

Mr. London is an author, illustrator, designer, part-time Samurai, Army veteran,
former rocket scientist, and tank blower-upper. He blatantly violates child labor
laws by forcing his three young sons to read his silly books and tests bad jokes on
them without proper protective gear.

Table of Contents

A Note on STEM and Chemistry
STEM stands for science, technology, engineering, and mathematics. In this book, you will learn about acids, bases, reactions, and solutions. While mixing acids and bases may look like fun, do not attempt to mix any chemicals together unless under the supervision of a chemistry teacher.

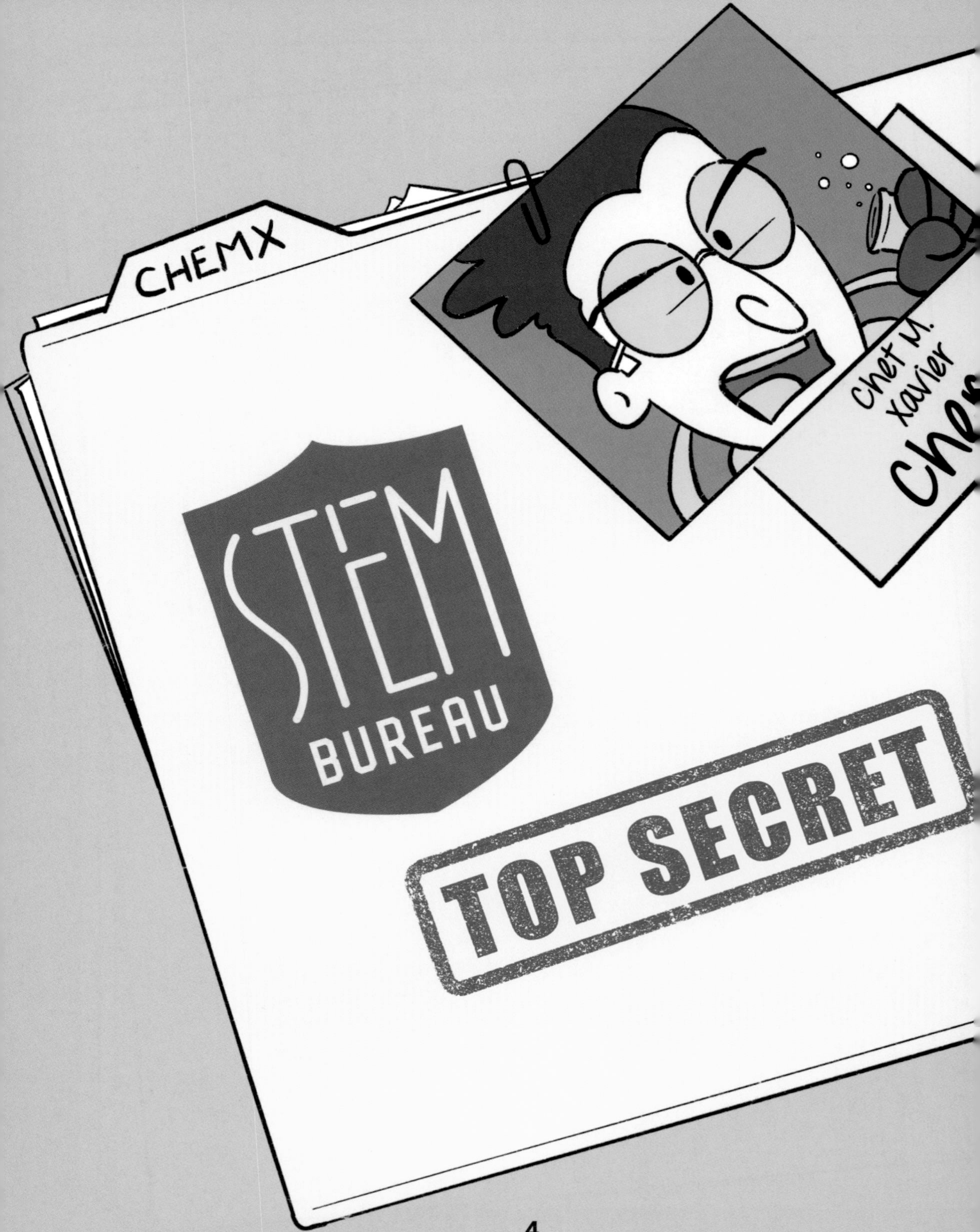
CHEMX
Chet M. Xavier
STEM BUREAU
TOP SECRET

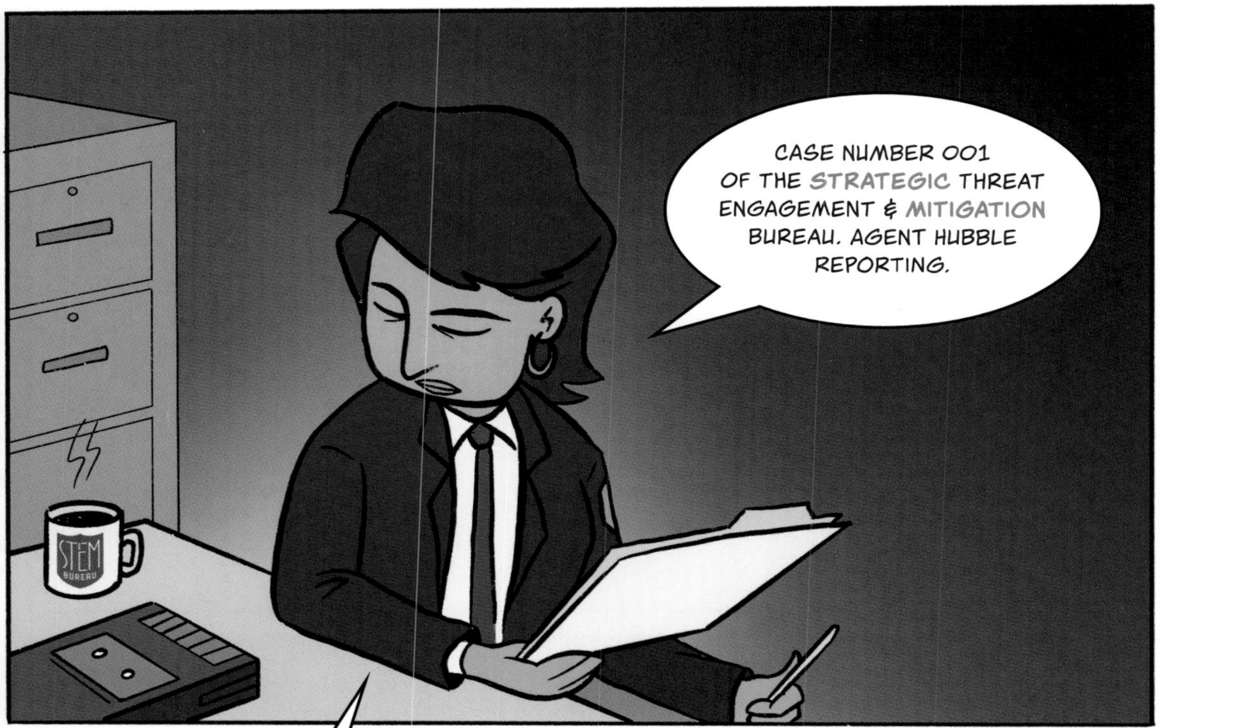
CASE NUMBER 001 OF THE STRATEGIC THREAT ENGAGEMENT & MITIGATION BUREAU. AGENT HUBBLE REPORTING.
STEM BUREAU

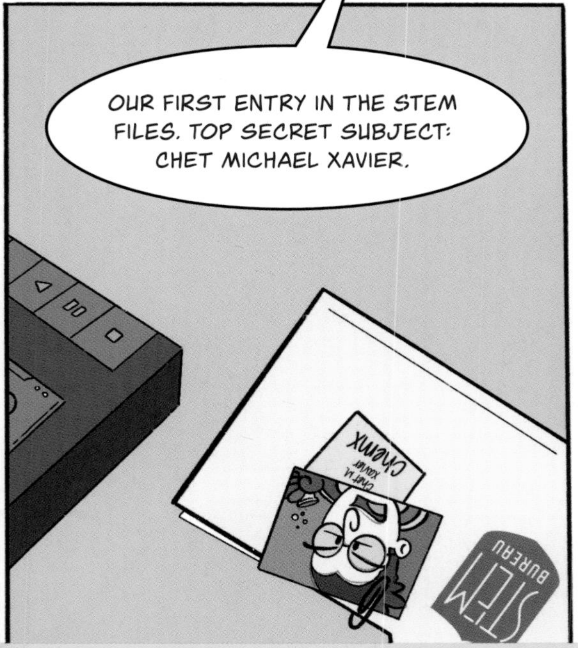
OUR FIRST ENTRY IN THE STEM FILES. TOP SECRET SUBJECT: CHET MICHAEL XAVIER.

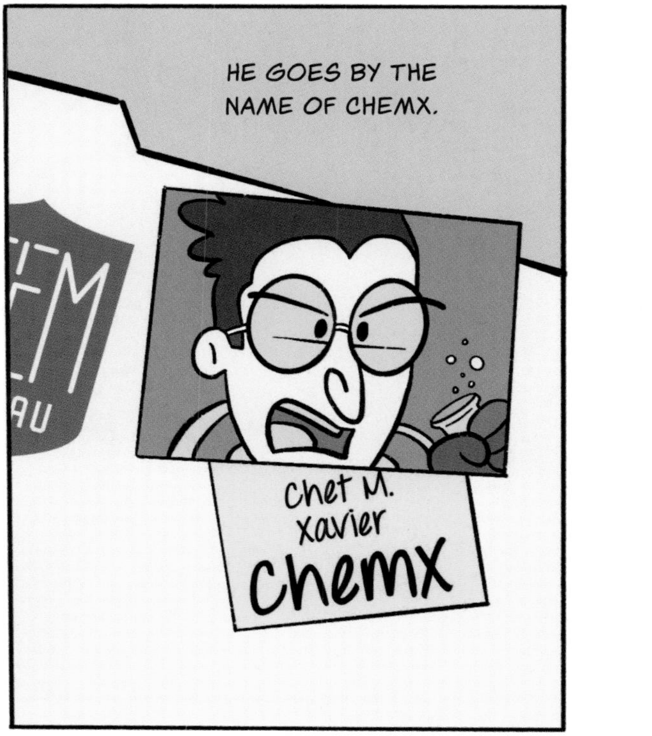
HE GOES BY THE NAME OF CHEMX.
Chet M. Xavier
Chemx

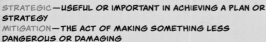

STRATEGIC—USEFUL OR IMPORTANT IN ACHIEVING A PLAN OR STRATEGY
MITIGATION—THE ACT OF MAKING SOMETHING LESS DANGEROUS OR DAMAGING

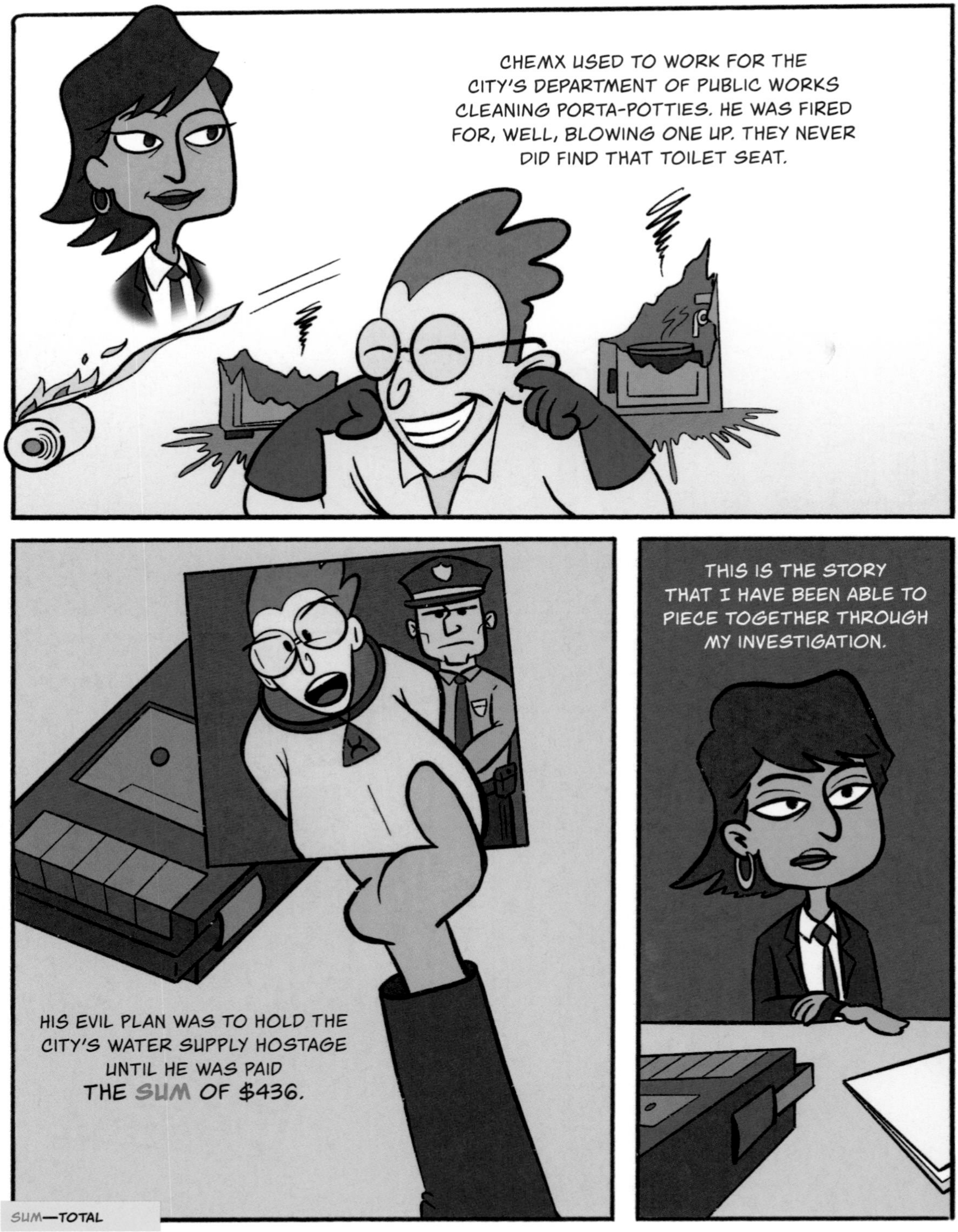
CHEMX USED TO WORK FOR THE CITY'S DEPARTMENT OF PUBLIC WORKS CLEANING PORTA-POTTIES. HE WAS FIRED FOR, WELL, BLOWING ONE UP. THEY NEVER DID FIND THAT TOILET SEAT.
HIS EVIL PLAN WAS TO HOLD THE CITY'S WATER SUPPLY HOSTAGE UNTIL HE WAS PAID THE SUM OF $436.
THIS IS THE STORY THAT I HAVE BEEN ABLE TO PIECE TOGETHER THROUGH MY INVESTIGATION.
SUM—TOTAL

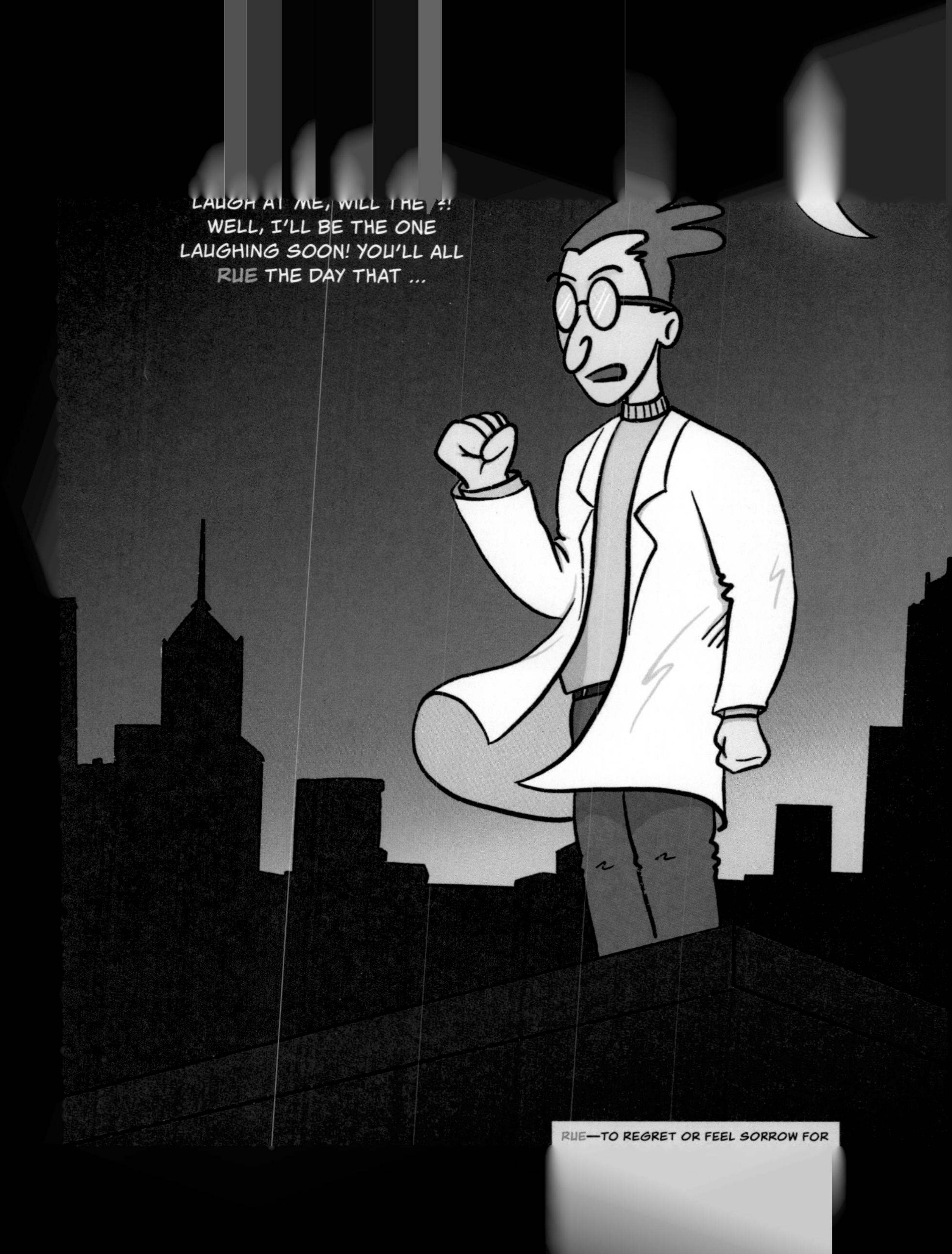
LAUGH AT ME, WILL THE ?!
WELL, I'LL BE THE ONE LAUGHING SOON! YOU'LL ALL RUE THE DAY THAT ...

RUE—TO REGRET OR FEEL SORROW FOR

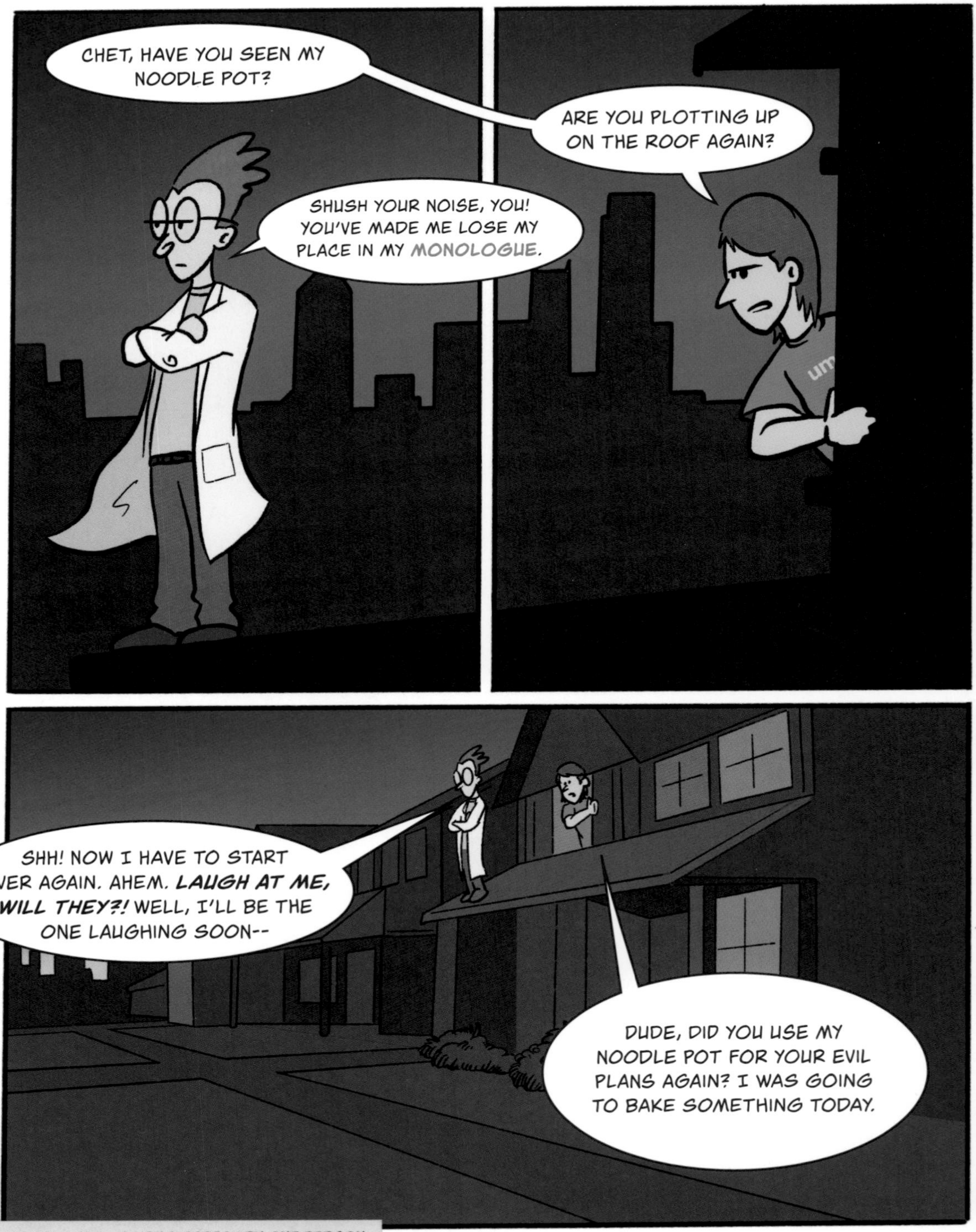
CHET, HAVE YOU SEEN MY NOODLE POT?
ARE YOU PLOTTING UP ON THE ROOF AGAIN?
SHUSH YOUR NOISE, YOU! YOU'VE MADE ME LOSE MY PLACE IN MY MONOLOGUE.
SHH! NOW I HAVE TO START OVER AGAIN. AHEM. LAUGH AT ME, WILL THEY?! WELL, I'LL BE THE ONE LAUGHING SOON--
DUDE, DID YOU USE MY NOODLE POT FOR YOUR EVIL PLANS AGAIN? I WAS GOING TO BAKE SOMETHING TODAY.

MONOLOGUE—**A LONG SPEECH BY ONE PERSON**

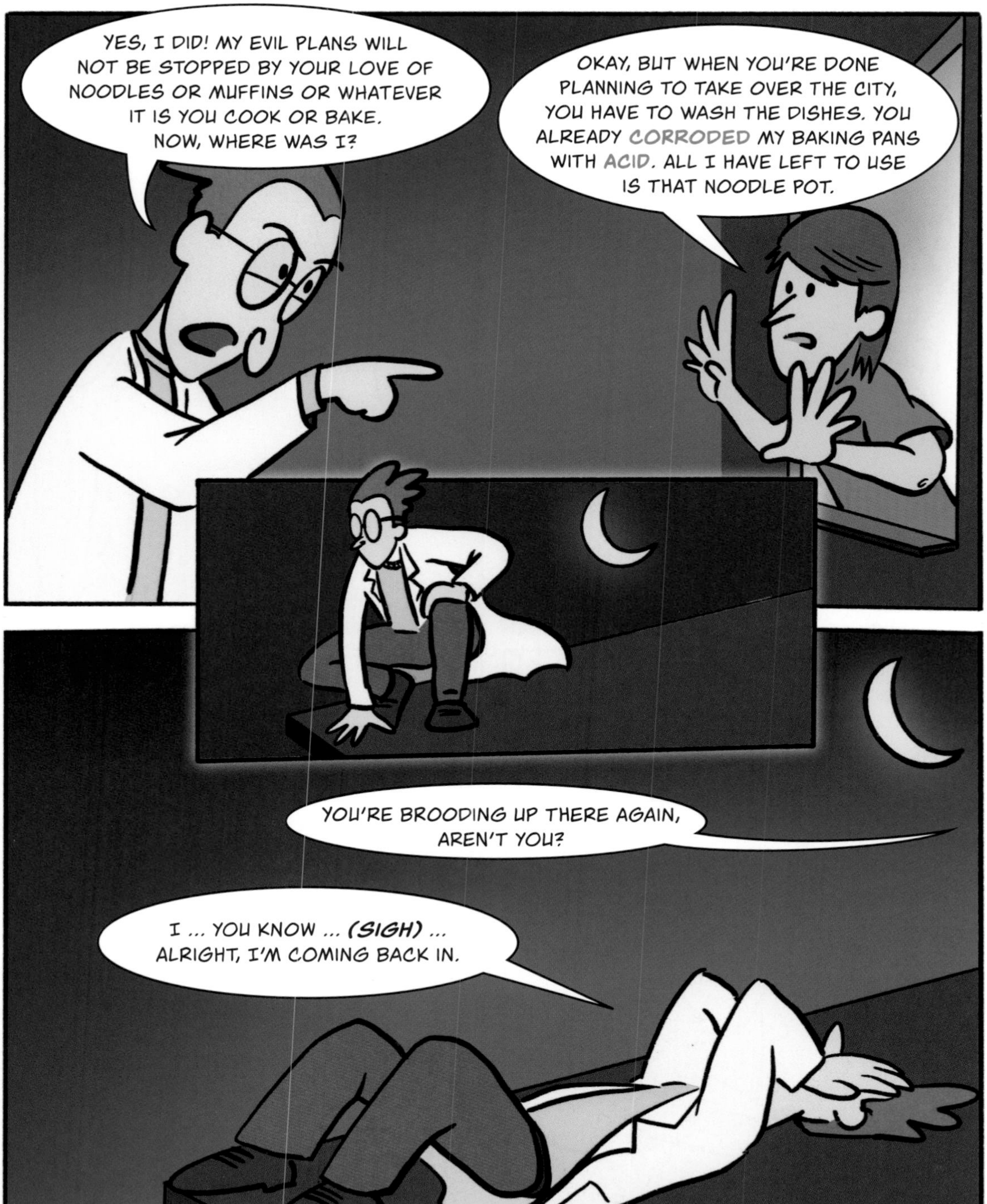
YES, I DID! MY EVIL PLANS WILL NOT BE STOPPED BY YOUR LOVE OF NOODLES OR MUFFINS OR WHATEVER IT IS YOU COOK OR BAKE. NOW, WHERE WAS I?
OKAY, BUT WHEN YOU'RE DONE PLANNING TO TAKE OVER THE CITY, YOU HAVE TO WASH THE DISHES. YOU ALREADY CORRODED MY BAKING PANS WITH ACID. ALL I HAVE LEFT TO USE IS THAT NOODLE POT.
YOU'RE BROODING UP THERE AGAIN, AREN'T YOU?
I ... YOU KNOW ... (SIGH) ... ALRIGHT, I'M COMING BACK IN.

CORRODED—TO CAUSE TO BREAK APART SLOWLY AND BE DESTROYED THROUGH A CHEMICAL PROCESS

ACID—A CHEMICAL SUBSTANCE THAT DISSOLVES SOME METALS AND CAN BURN SKIN

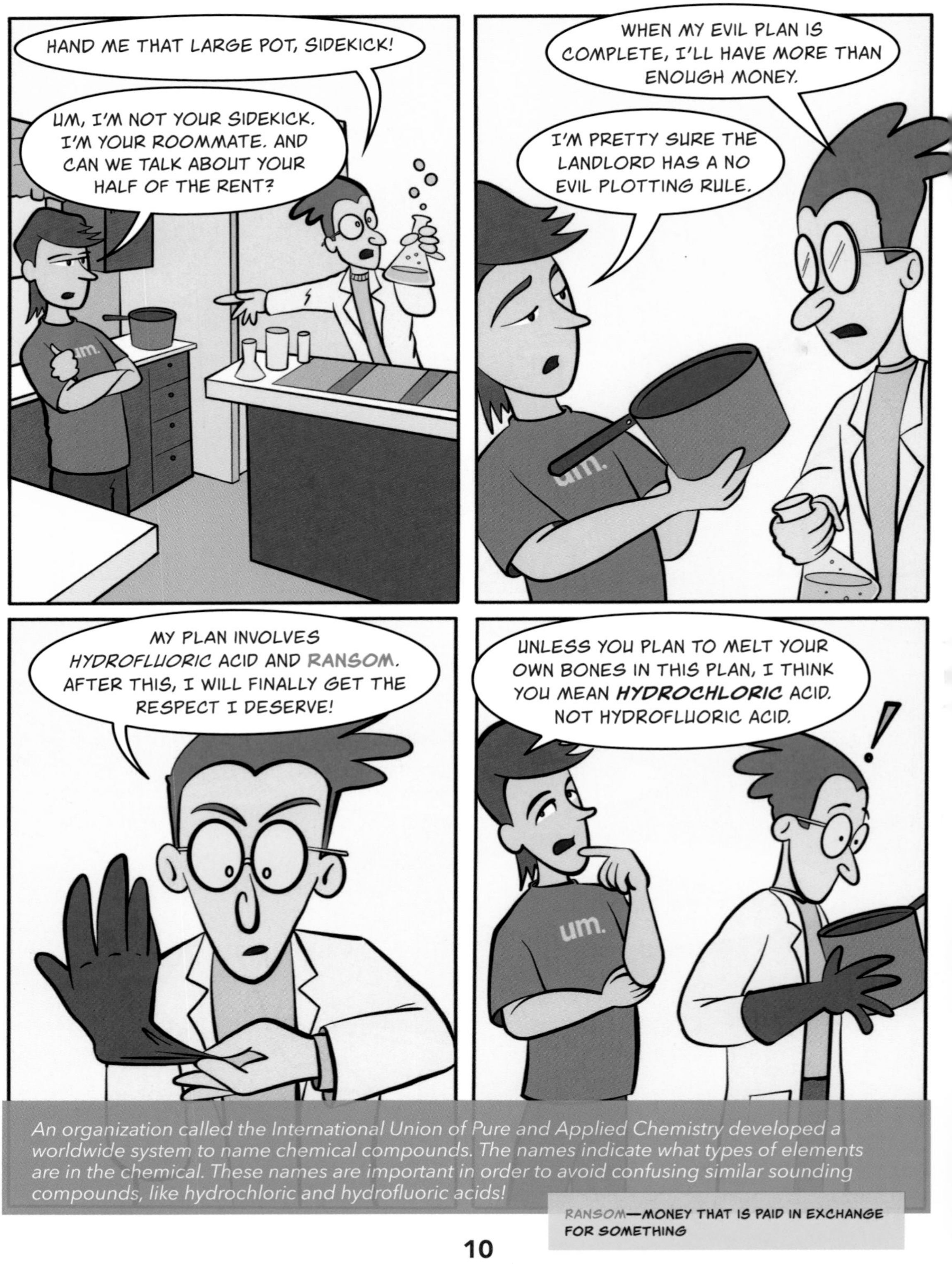
HAND ME THAT LARGE POT, SIDEKICK!
UM, I'M NOT YOUR SIDEKICK. I'M YOUR ROOMMATE. AND CAN WE TALK ABOUT YOUR HALF OF THE RENT?
WHEN MY EVIL PLAN IS COMPLETE, I'LL HAVE MORE THAN ENOUGH MONEY.
I'M PRETTY SURE THE LANDLORD HAS A NO EVIL PLOTTING RULE.
MY PLAN INVOLVES *HYDROFLUORIC* ACID AND **RANSOM**. AFTER THIS, I WILL FINALLY GET THE RESPECT I DESERVE!
UNLESS YOU PLAN TO MELT YOUR OWN BONES IN THIS PLAN, I THINK YOU MEAN ***HYDROCHLORIC*** ACID. NOT HYDROFLUORIC ACID.
!

An organization called the International Union of Pure and Applied Chemistry developed a worldwide system to name chemical compounds. The names indicate what types of elements are in the chemical. These names are important in order to avoid confusing similar sounding compounds, like hydrochloric and hydrofluoric acids!

RANSOM—MONEY THAT IS PAID IN EXCHANGE FOR SOMETHING

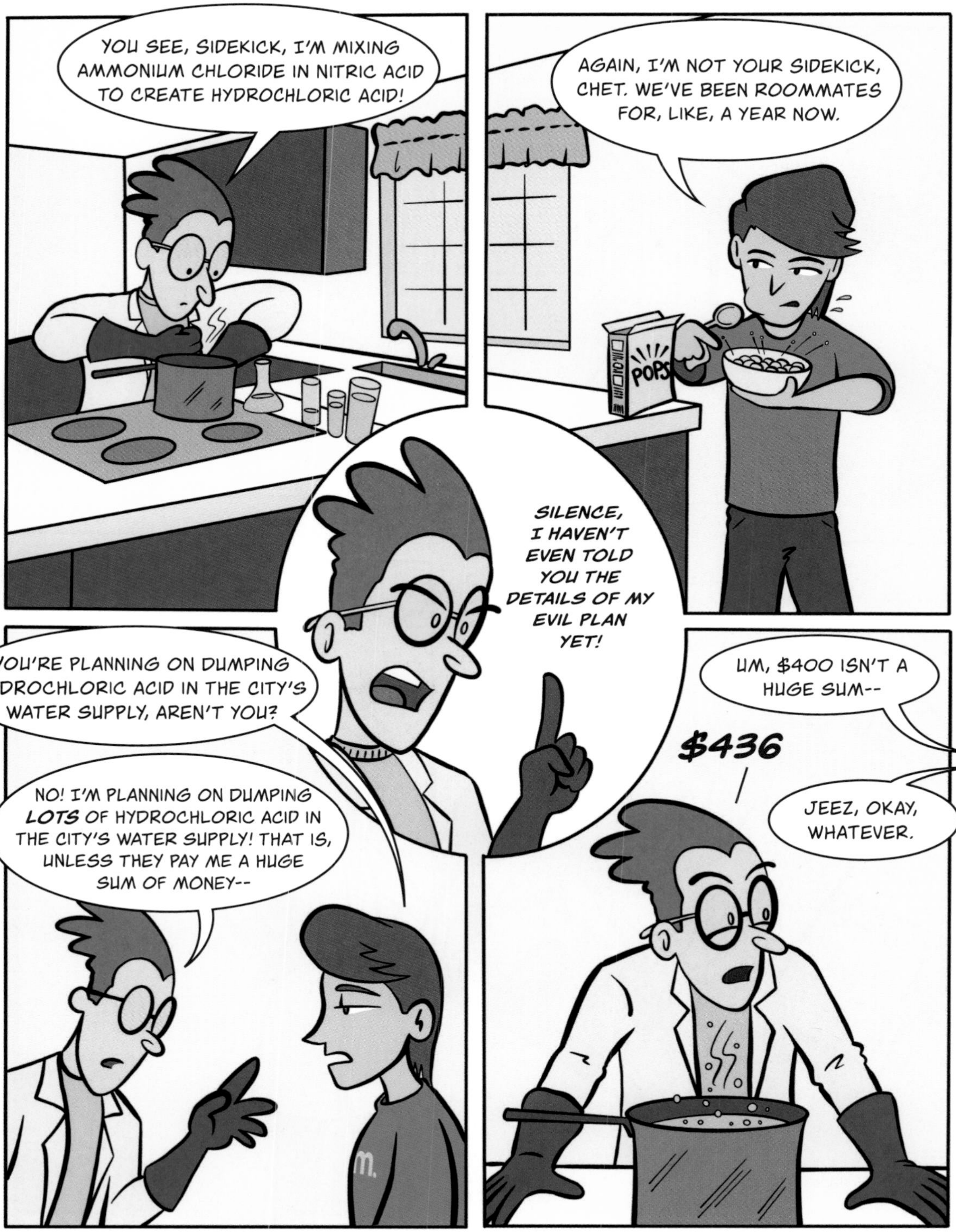
YOU SEE, SIDEKICK, I'M MIXING AMMONIUM CHLORIDE IN NITRIC ACID TO CREATE HYDROCHLORIC ACID!
AGAIN, I'M NOT YOUR SIDEKICK, CHET. WE'VE BEEN ROOMMATES FOR, LIKE, A YEAR NOW.
POPS
SILENCE, I HAVEN'T EVEN TOLD YOU THE DETAILS OF MY EVIL PLAN YET!
YOU'RE PLANNING ON DUMPING HYDROCHLORIC ACID IN THE CITY'S WATER SUPPLY, AREN'T YOU?
NO! I'M PLANNING ON DUMPING LOTS OF HYDROCHLORIC ACID IN THE CITY'S WATER SUPPLY! THAT IS, UNLESS THEY PAY ME A HUGE SUM OF MONEY--
$436
UM, $400 ISN'T A HUGE SUM--
JEEZ, OKAY, WHATEVER.

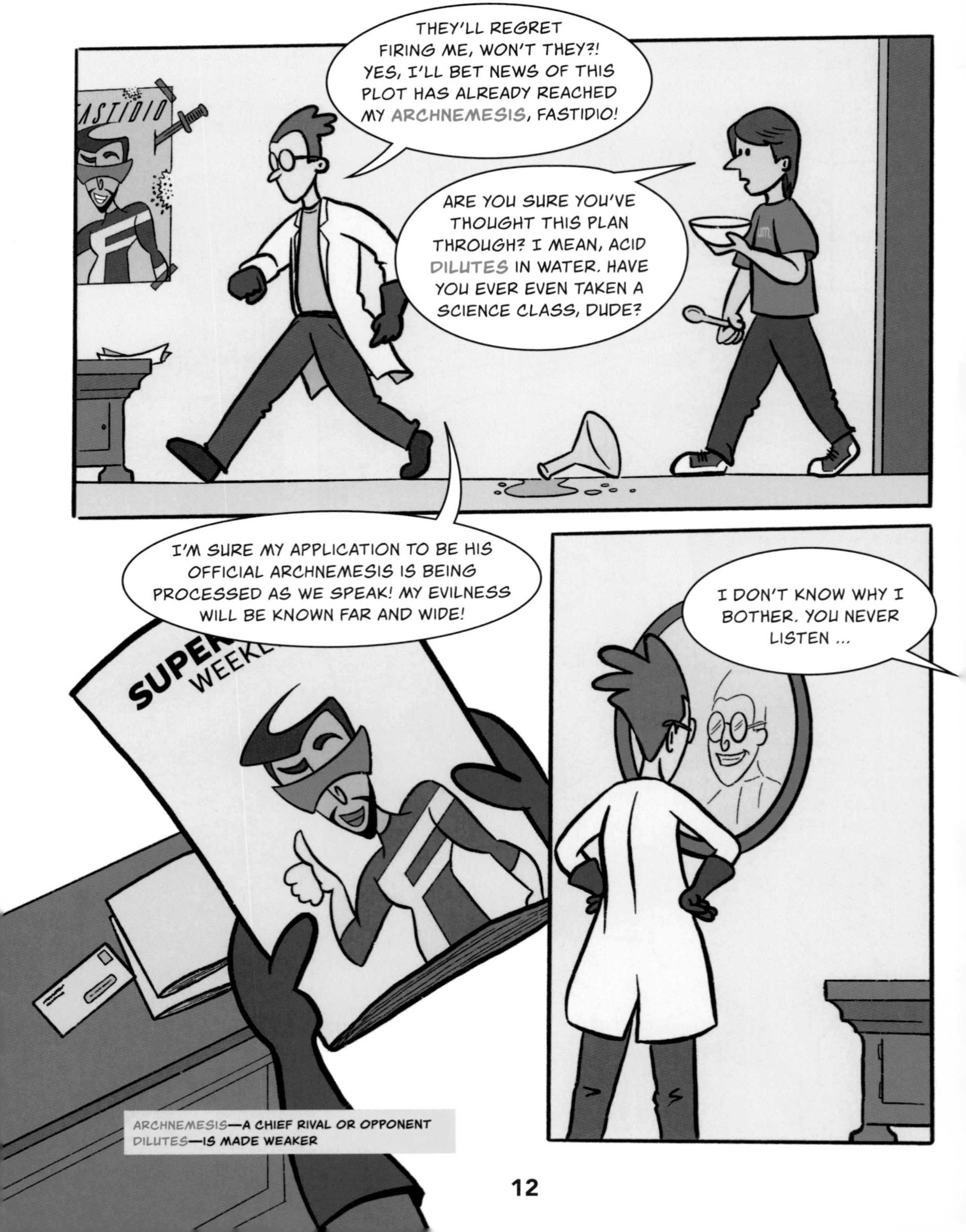
THEY'LL REGRET FIRING ME, WON'T THEY?! YES, I'LL BET NEWS OF THIS PLOT HAS ALREADY REACHED MY ARCHNEMESIS, FASTIDIO!
ARE YOU SURE YOU'VE THOUGHT THIS PLAN THROUGH? I MEAN, ACID DILUTES IN WATER. HAVE YOU EVER EVEN TAKEN A SCIENCE CLASS, DUDE?
I'M SURE MY APPLICATION TO BE HIS OFFICIAL ARCHNEMESIS IS BEING PROCESSED AS WE SPEAK! MY EVILNESS WILL BE KNOWN FAR AND WIDE!
I DON'T KNOW WHY I BOTHER. YOU NEVER LISTEN ...

ARCHNEMESIS—A CHIEF RIVAL OR OPPONENT
DILUTES—IS MADE WEAKER

Acids and Bases— What Are They?

All liquids have acidic or basic traits. In chemistry, these traits play an important role in chemical reactions. To figure out if a liquid is acidic or basic, you need to know if the liquid is willing to give away hydrogen ions (H+) or hydroxide ions (OH-). Acids like to give away H+ ions, while bases like to give away OH- ions. Scientists use a pH scale to measure how basic or acidic a liquid is. This scale ranges from 0 to 14. If a liquid has a pH below 7, the liquid has acidic traits. If a liquid has a pH above 7, the liquid has basic traits.

um.

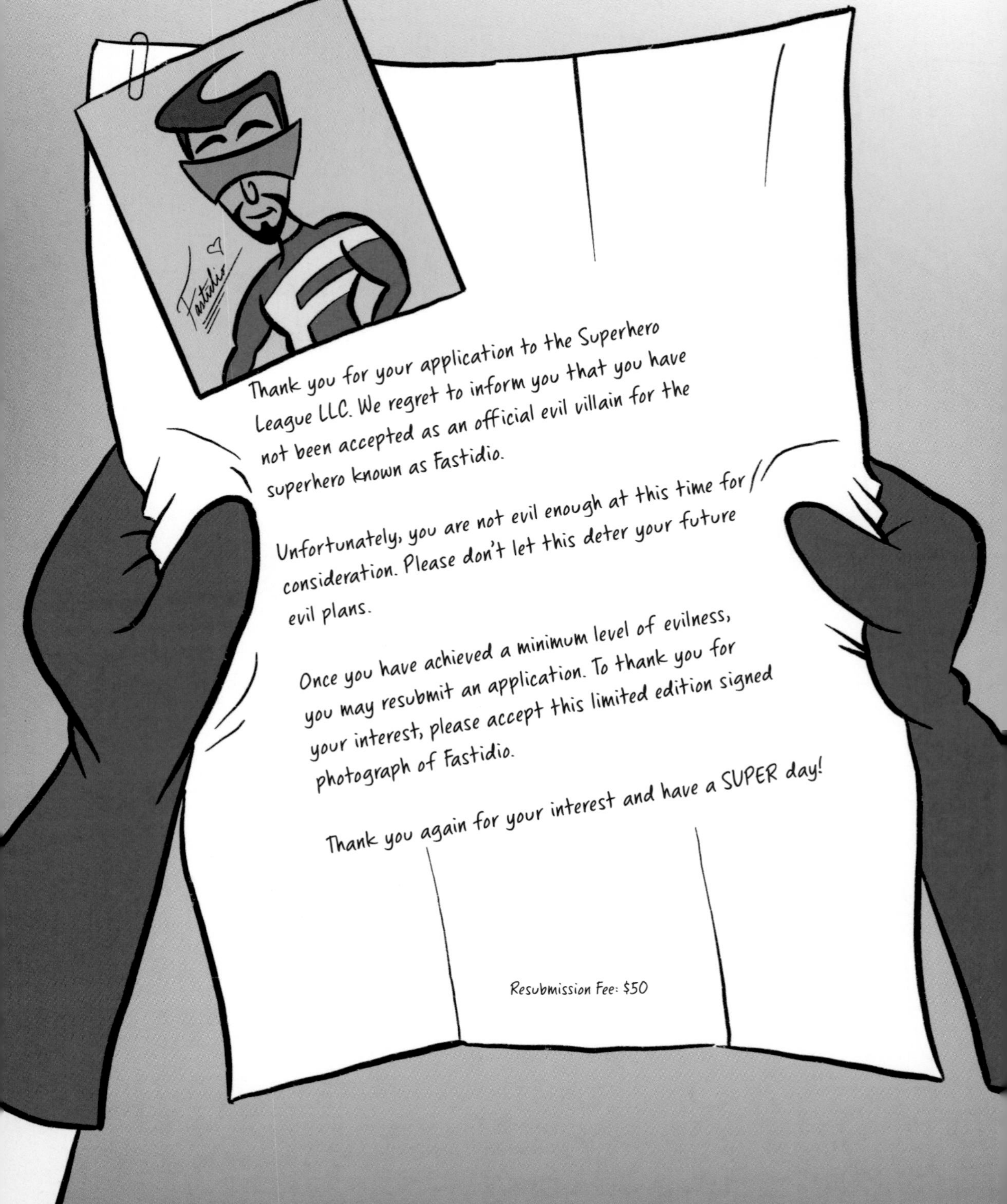
Fastidio
Thank you for your application to the Superhero League LLC. We regret to inform you that you have not been accepted as an official evil villain for the superhero known as Fastidio.
Unfortunately, you are not evil enough at this time for consideration. Please don't let this deter your future evil plans.
Once you have achieved a minimum level of evilness, you may resubmit an application. To thank you for your interest, please accept this limited edition signed photograph of Fastidio.
Thank you again for your interest and have a SUPER day!
Resubmission Fee: $50

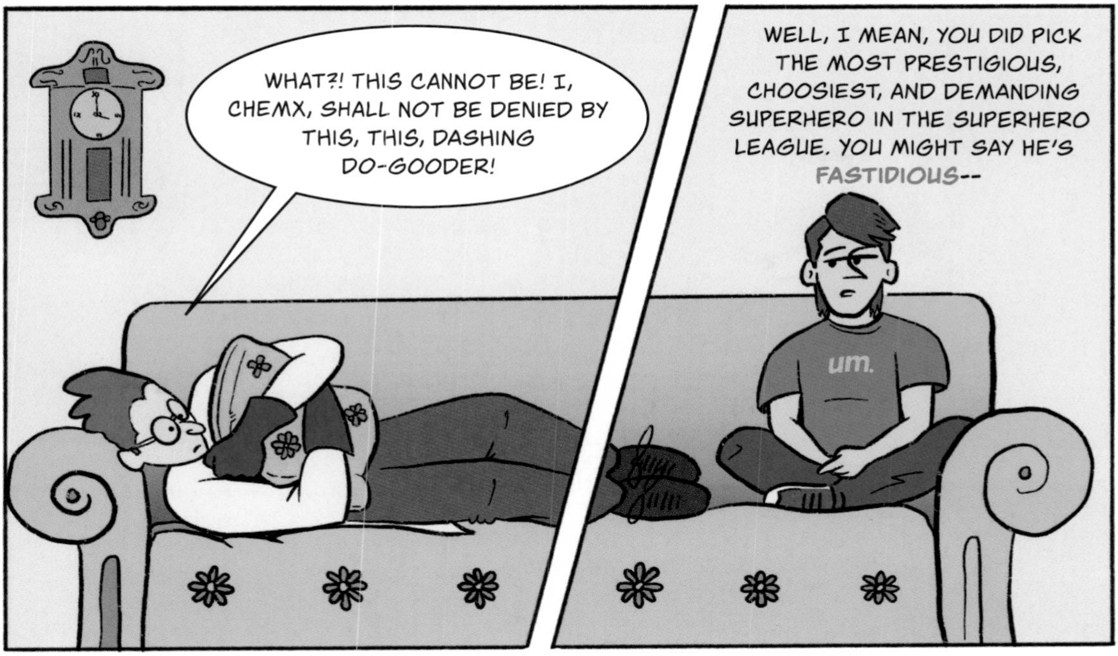

WHAT?! THIS CANNOT BE! I, CHEMX, SHALL NOT BE DENIED BY THIS, THIS, DASHING DO-GOODER!
WELL, I MEAN, YOU DID PICK THE MOST PRESTIGIOUS, CHOOSIEST, AND DEMANDING SUPERHERO IN THE SUPERHERO LEAGUE. YOU MIGHT SAY HE'S FASTIDIOUS--
um.

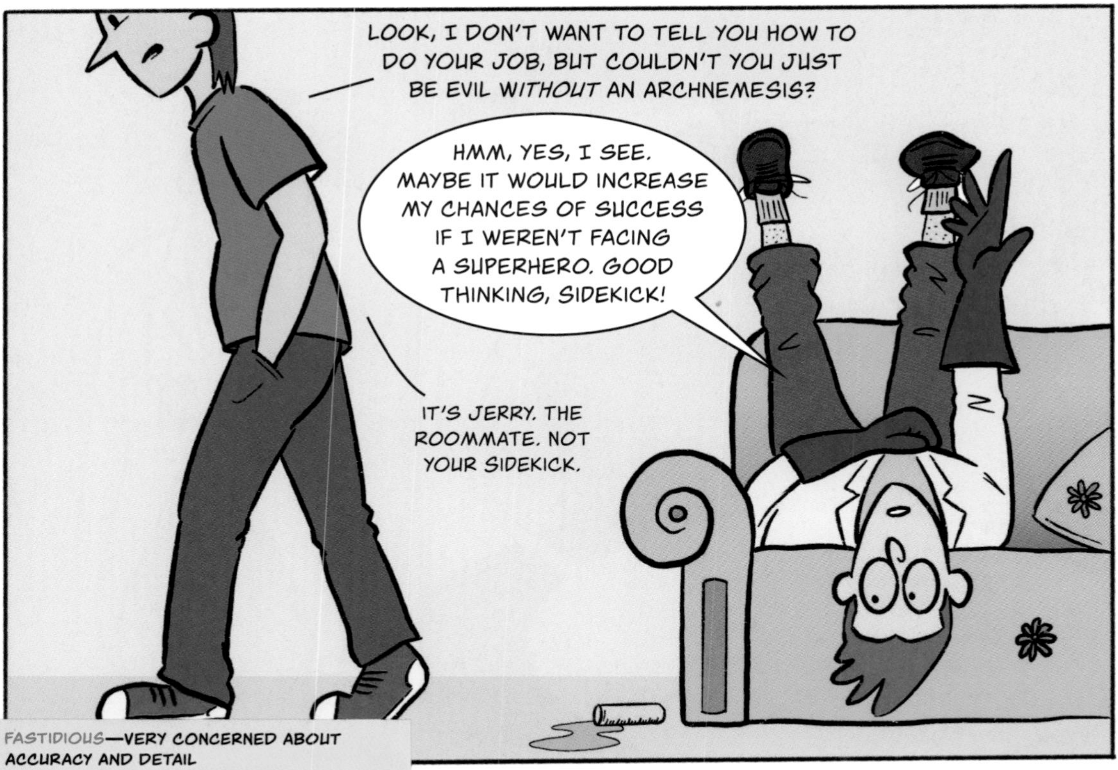

LOOK, I DON'T WANT TO TELL YOU HOW TO DO YOUR JOB, BUT COULDN'T YOU JUST BE EVIL *WITHOUT* AN ARCHNEMESIS?
HMM, YES, I SEE. MAYBE IT WOULD INCREASE MY CHANCES OF SUCCESS IF I WEREN'T FACING A SUPERHERO. GOOD THINKING, SIDEKICK!
IT'S JERRY. THE ROOMMATE. NOT YOUR SIDEKICK.

FASTIDIOUS—VERY CONCERNED ABOUT ACCURACY AND DETAIL

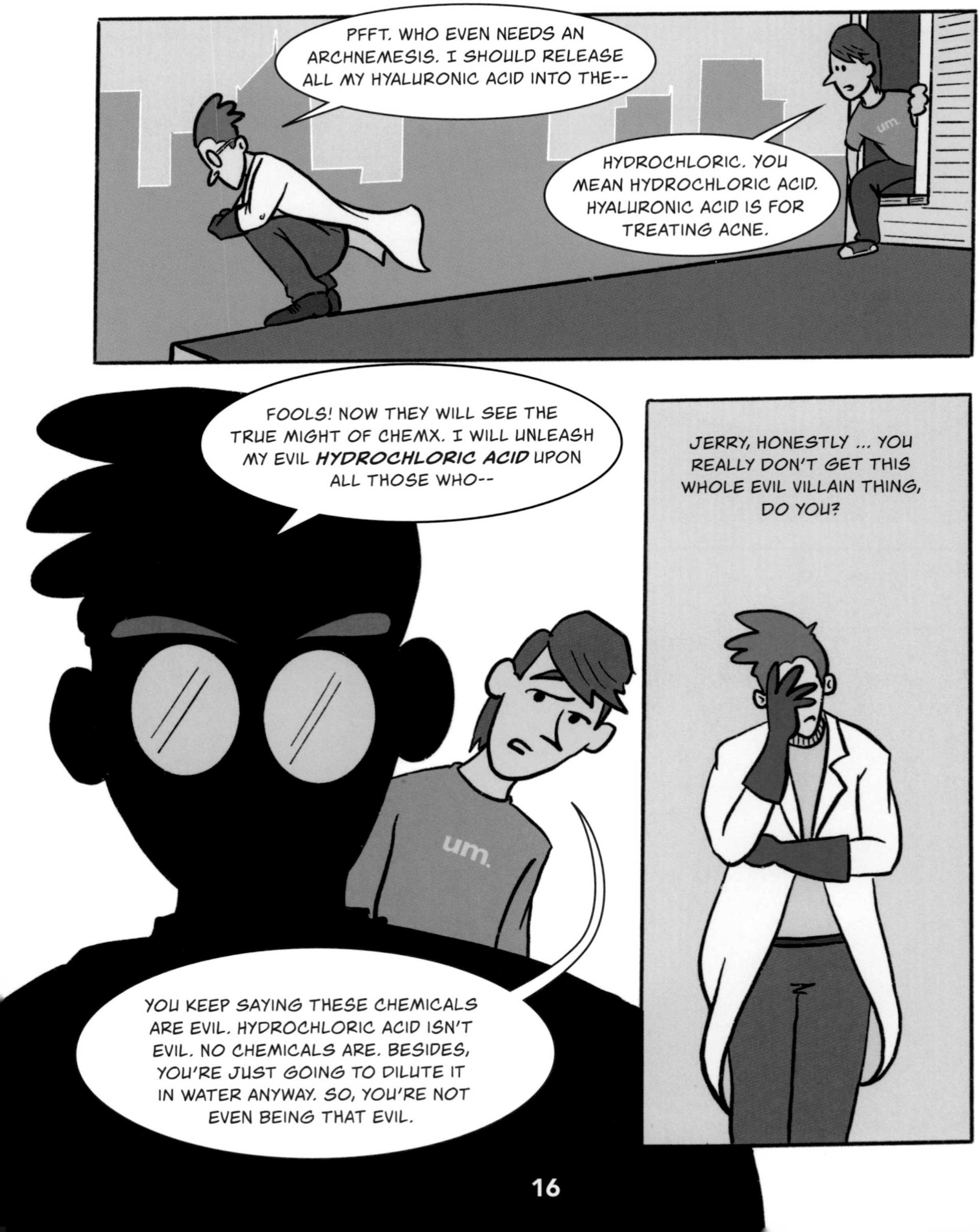
PFFT. WHO EVEN NEEDS AN ARCHNEMESIS. I SHOULD RELEASE ALL MY HYALURONIC ACID INTO THE--
HYDROCHLORIC. YOU MEAN HYDROCHLORIC ACID. HYALURONIC ACID IS FOR TREATING ACNE.
FOOLS! NOW THEY WILL SEE THE TRUE MIGHT OF CHEMX. I WILL UNLEASH MY EVIL ***HYDROCHLORIC ACID*** UPON ALL THOSE WHO--
YOU KEEP SAYING THESE CHEMICALS ARE EVIL. HYDROCHLORIC ACID ISN'T EVIL. NO CHEMICALS ARE. BESIDES, YOU'RE JUST GOING TO DILUTE IT IN WATER ANYWAY. SO, YOU'RE NOT EVEN BEING THAT EVIL.
JERRY, HONESTLY ... YOU REALLY DON'T GET THIS WHOLE EVIL VILLAIN THING, DO YOU?

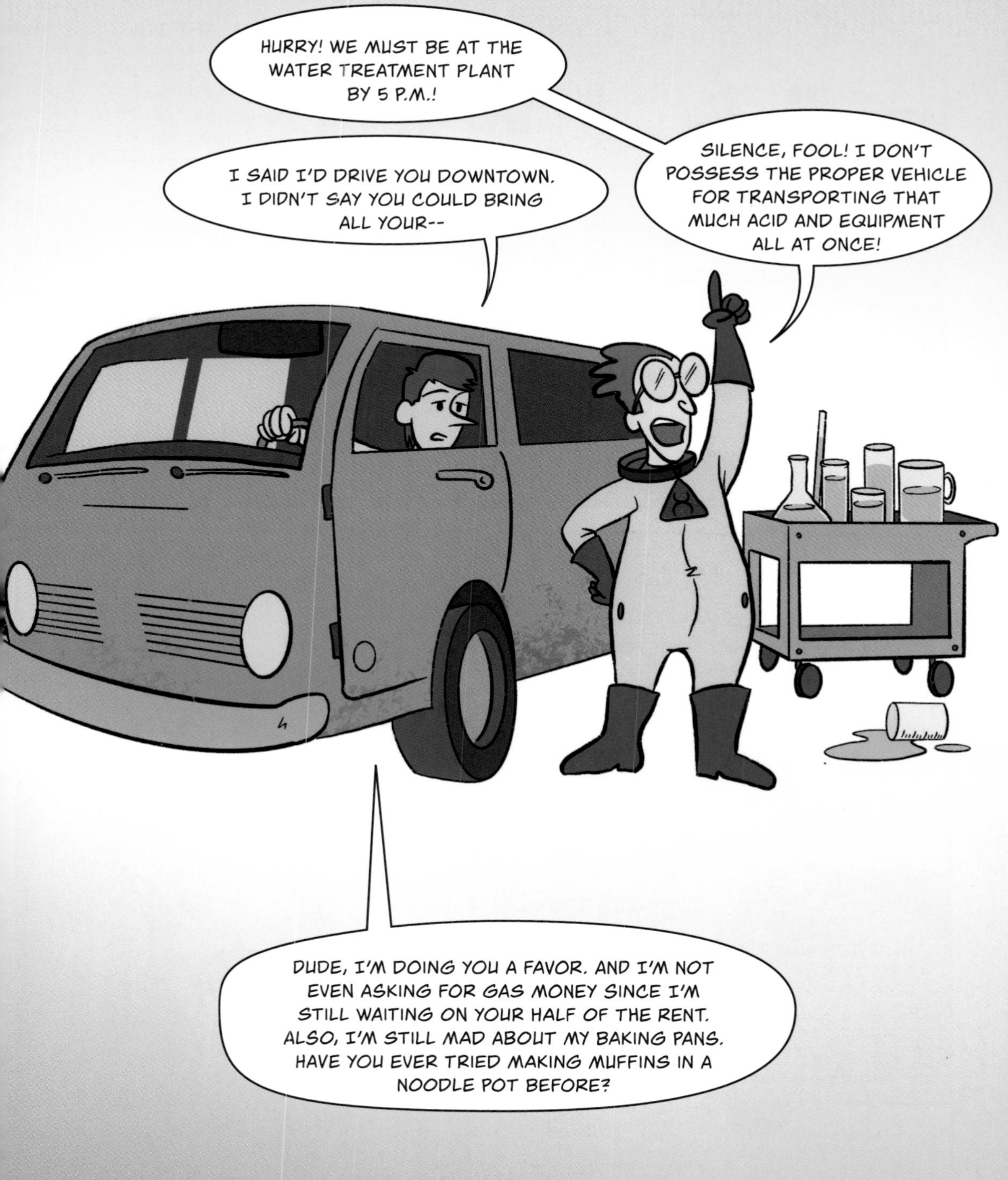
HURRY! WE MUST BE AT THE WATER TREATMENT PLANT BY 5 P.M.!
I SAID I'D DRIVE YOU DOWNTOWN. I DIDN'T SAY YOU COULD BRING ALL YOUR--
SILENCE, FOOL! I DON'T POSSESS THE PROPER VEHICLE FOR TRANSPORTING THAT MUCH ACID AND EQUIPMENT ALL AT ONCE!
DUDE, I'M DOING YOU A FAVOR. AND I'M NOT EVEN ASKING FOR GAS MONEY SINCE I'M STILL WAITING ON YOUR HALF OF THE RENT. ALSO, I'M STILL MAD ABOUT MY BAKING PANS. HAVE YOU EVER TRIED MAKING MUFFINS IN A NOODLE POT BEFORE?

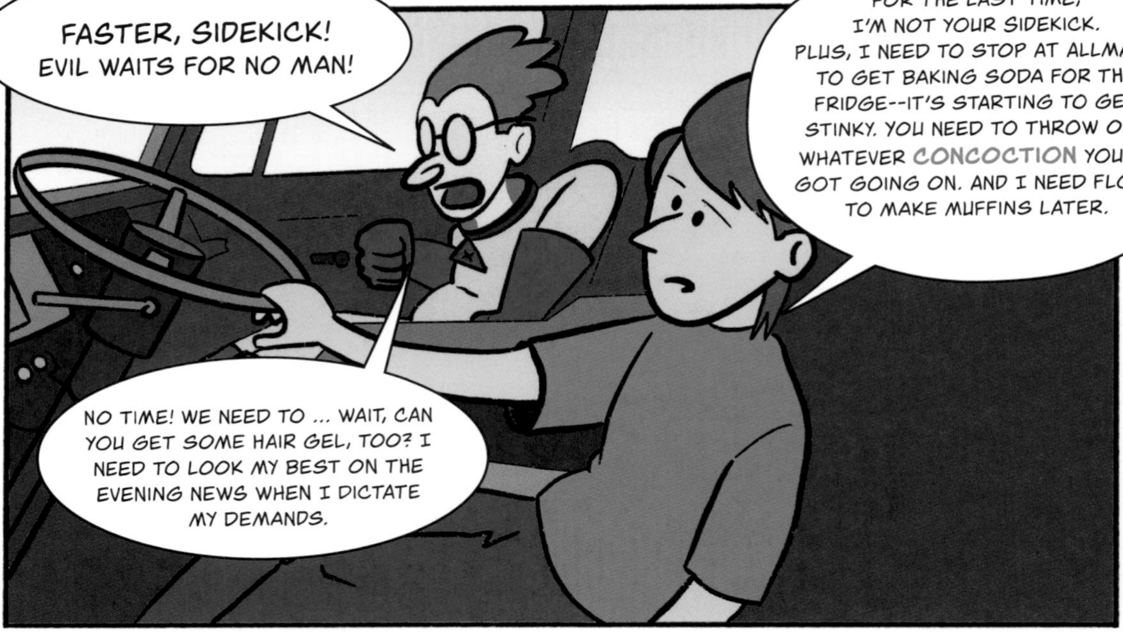
FASTER, SIDEKICK! EVIL WAITS FOR NO MAN!
FOR THE LAST TIME, I'M NOT YOUR SIDEKICK. PLUS, I NEED TO STOP AT ALLMA TO GET BAKING SODA FOR THE FRIDGE--IT'S STARTING TO GET STINKY. YOU NEED TO THROW OU WHATEVER CONCOCTION YOU' GOT GOING ON. AND I NEED FLO TO MAKE MUFFINS LATER.
NO TIME! WE NEED TO ... WAIT, CAN YOU GET SOME HAIR GEL, TOO? I NEED TO LOOK MY BEST ON THE EVENING NEWS WHEN I DICTATE MY DEMANDS.

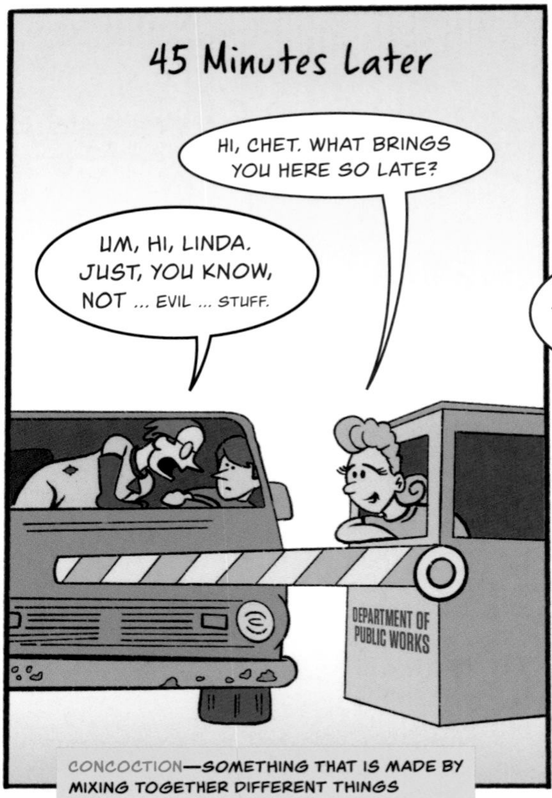
45 Minutes Later
HI, CHET. WHAT BRINGS YOU HERE SO LATE?
UM, HI, LINDA. JUST, YOU KNOW, NOT ... EVIL ... STUFF.
DEPARTMENT OF PUBLIC WORKS

CONCOCTION—SOMETHING THAT IS MADE BY MIXING TOGETHER DIFFERENT THINGS

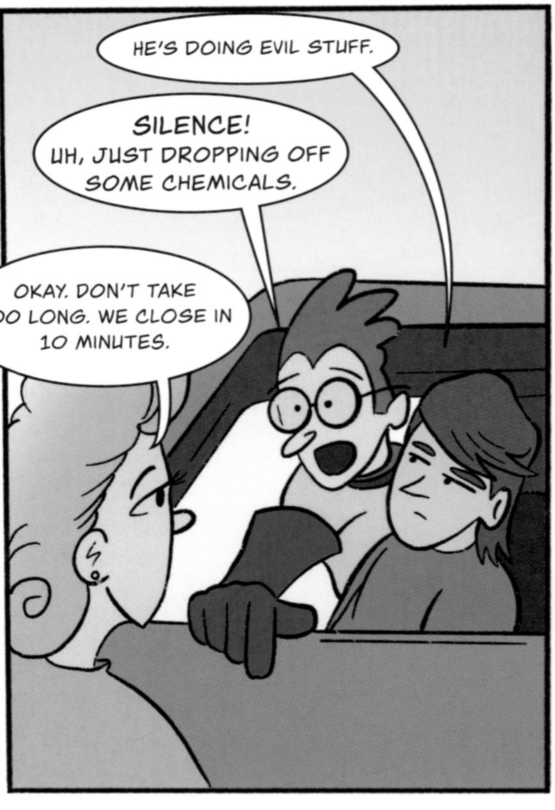
HE'S DOING EVIL STUFF.
SILENCE! UH, JUST DROPPING OFF SOME CHEMICALS.
OKAY. DON'T TAKE TOO LONG. WE CLOSE IN 10 MINUTES.

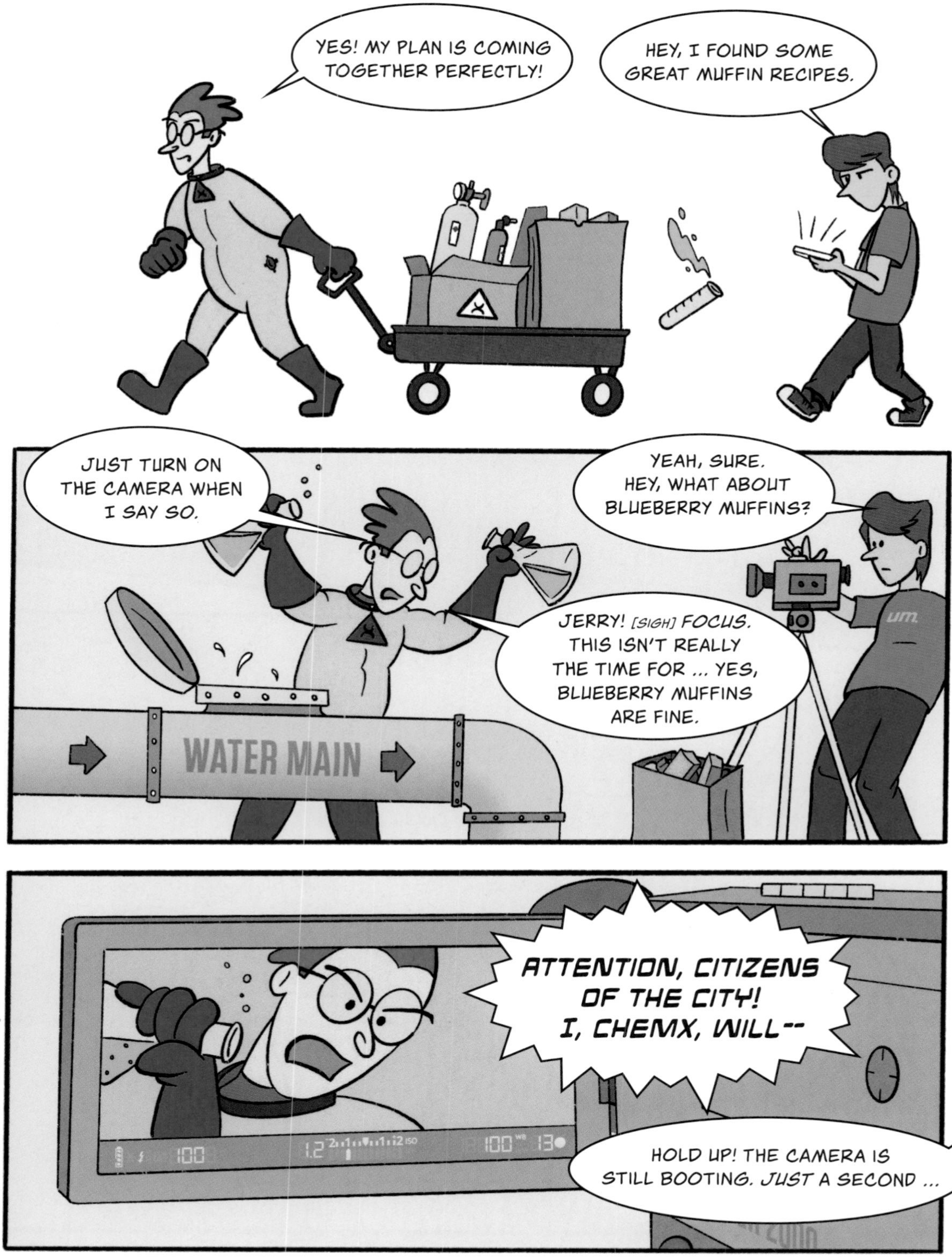

YES! MY PLAN IS COMING TOGETHER PERFECTLY!
HEY, I FOUND SOME GREAT MUFFIN RECIPES.
JUST TURN ON THE CAMERA WHEN I SAY SO.
YEAH, SURE. HEY, WHAT ABOUT BLUEBERRY MUFFINS?
JERRY! [SIGH] FOCUS. THIS ISN'T REALLY THE TIME FOR ... YES, BLUEBERRY MUFFINS ARE FINE.
WATER MAIN
UM
ATTENTION, CITIZENS OF THE CITY! I, CHEMX, WILL--
HOLD UP! THE CAMERA IS STILL BOOTING. JUST A SECOND ...

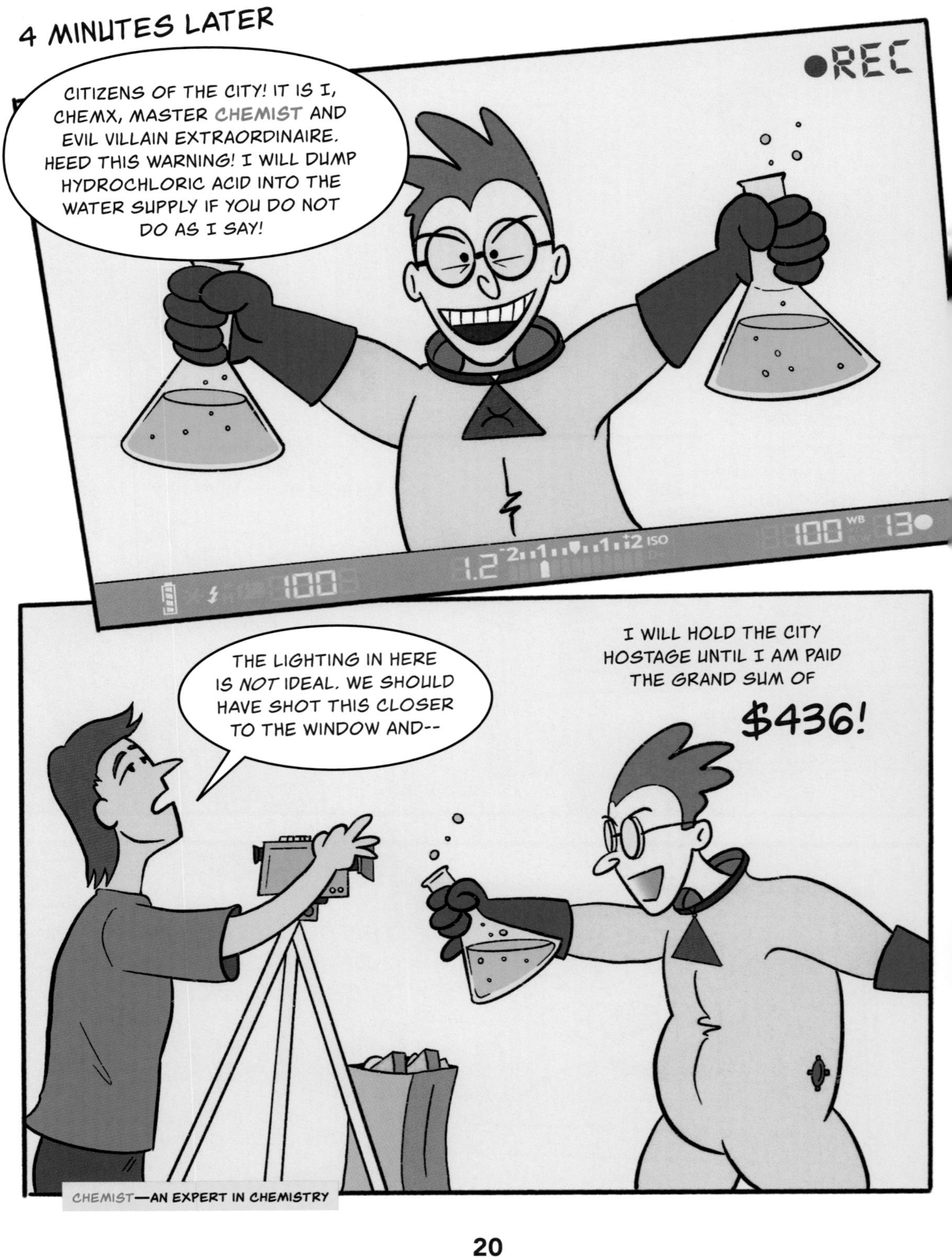
4 MINUTES LATER
REC
CITIZENS OF THE CITY! IT IS I, CHEMX, MASTER CHEMIST AND EVIL VILLAIN EXTRAORDINAIRE. HEED THIS WARNING! I WILL DUMP HYDROCHLORIC ACID INTO THE WATER SUPPLY IF YOU DO NOT DO AS I SAY!
THE LIGHTING IN HERE IS NOT IDEAL. WE SHOULD HAVE SHOT THIS CLOSER TO THE WINDOW AND--
I WILL HOLD THE CITY HOSTAGE UNTIL I AM PAID THE GRAND SUM OF
$436!

CHEMIST—AN EXPERT IN CHEMISTRY

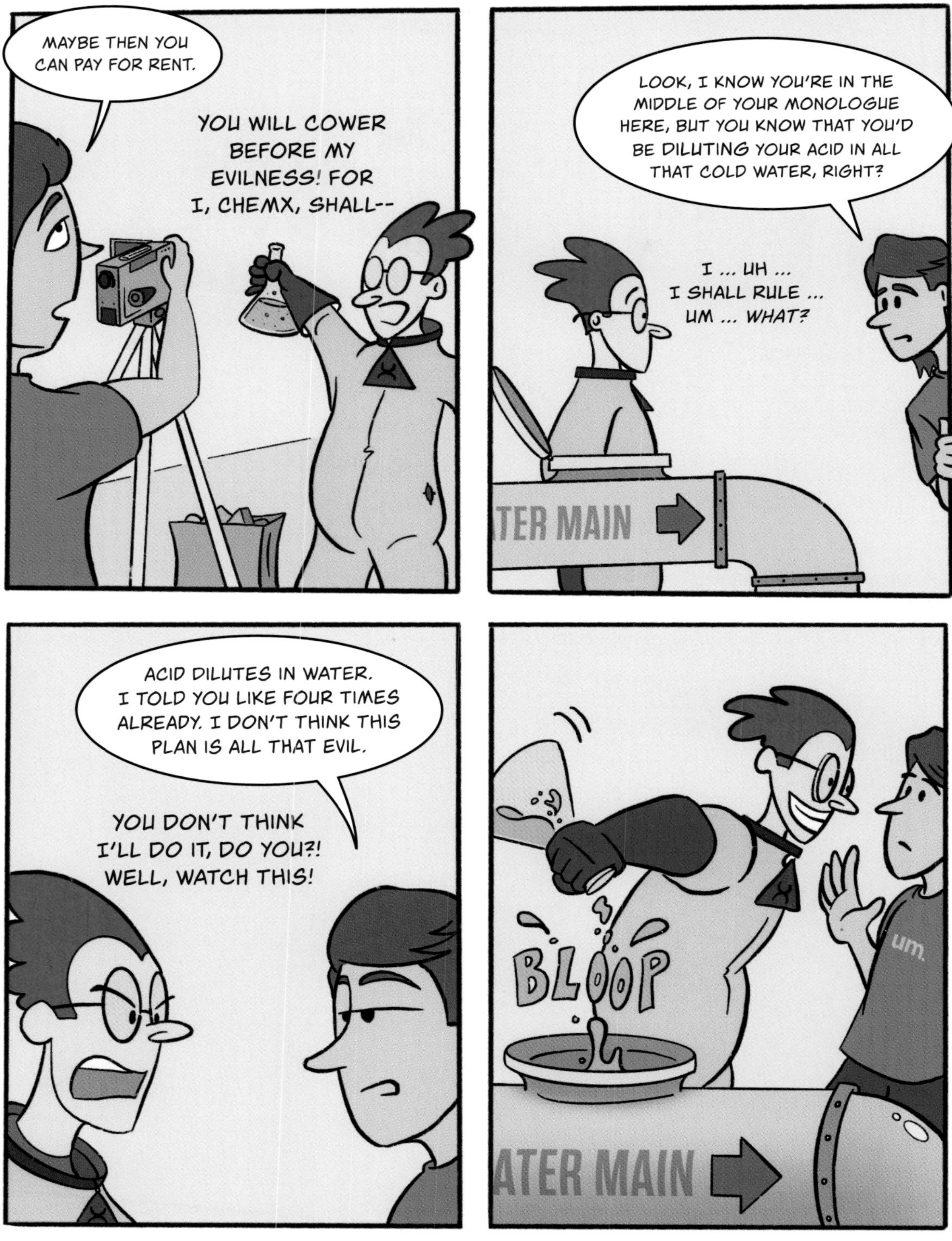
MAYBE THEN YOU CAN PAY FOR RENT.
YOU WILL COWER BEFORE MY EVILNESS! FOR I, CHEMX, SHALL--
LOOK, I KNOW YOU'RE IN THE MIDDLE OF YOUR MONOLOGUE HERE, BUT YOU KNOW THAT YOU'D BE DILUTING YOUR ACID IN ALL THAT COLD WATER, RIGHT?
I ... UH ... I SHALL RULE ... UM ... WHAT?
TER MAIN
ACID DILUTES IN WATER. I TOLD YOU LIKE FOUR TIMES ALREADY. I DON'T THINK THIS PLAN IS ALL THAT EVIL.
YOU DON'T THINK I'LL DO IT, DO YOU?! WELL, WATCH THIS!
BLOOP
um.
ATER MAIN

Hydrochloric Acid + Water + Baking Soda

Acids have a pH level below 7. This means acids like to give away hydrogen ions (H+). Since water is neutral and has a pH of 7, it can act like a base to accept H+ ions when reacting with an acid. When strong acids and strong bases react with each other, like hydrochloric acid (HCl) and Jerry's baking soda (sodium bicarbonate, NAHCO3), a neutralization reaction takes place. Neutralization reactions form water molecules by combining H+ ions and hydroxide ions (OH-). In ChemX's case, when hydrochloric acid reacts with baking soda in water, the result is water, carbon dioxide (CO2), and salt (sodium chloride, NaCl). These are all harmless by-products!

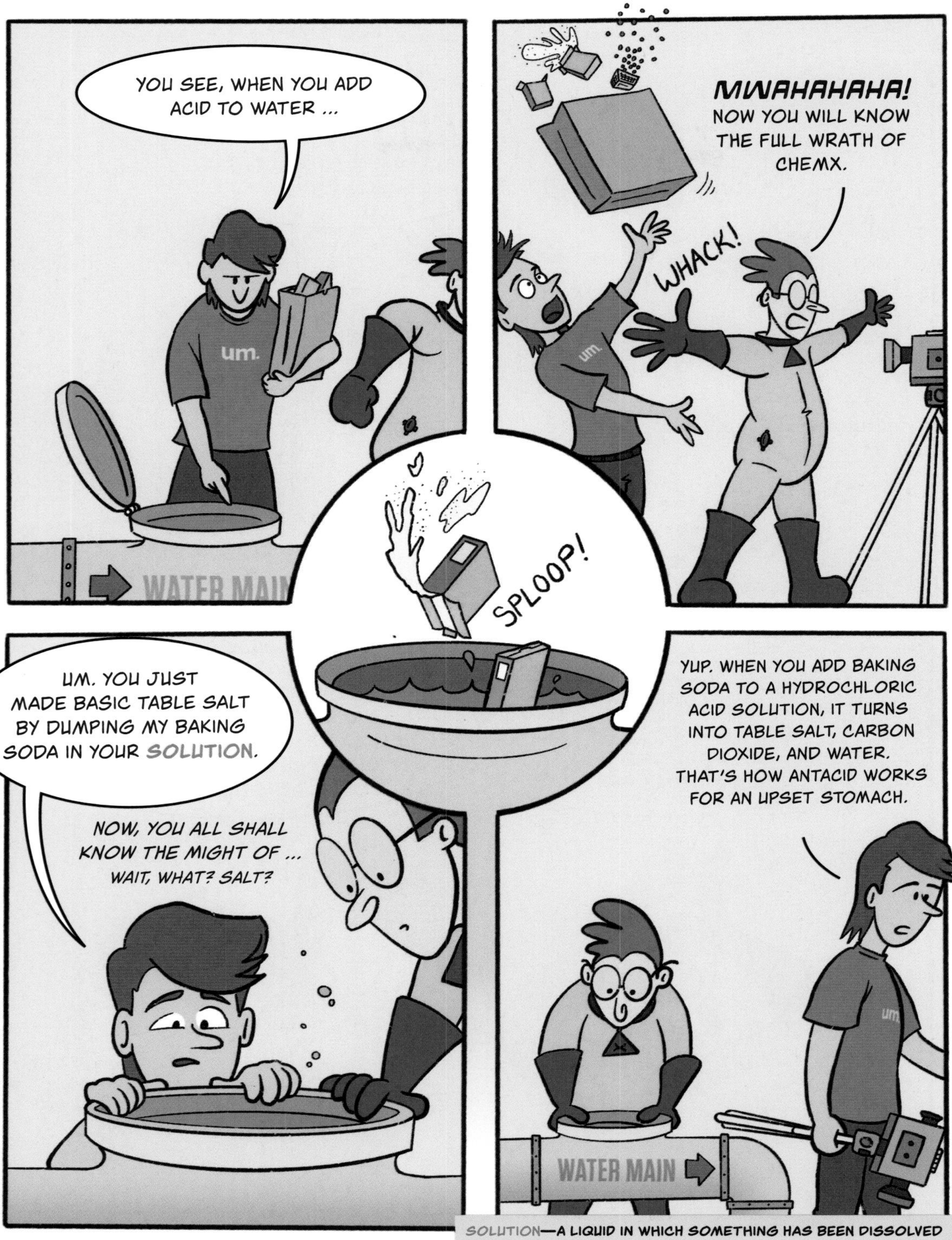

YOU SEE, WHEN YOU ADD ACID TO WATER ...
WATER MAIN
MWAHAHAHA! NOW YOU WILL KNOW THE FULL WRATH OF CHEMX.
WHACK!
um.
SPLOOP!
UM. YOU JUST MADE BASIC TABLE SALT BY DUMPING MY BAKING SODA IN YOUR SOLUTION.
NOW, YOU ALL SHALL KNOW THE MIGHT OF ... WAIT, WHAT? SALT?
YUP. WHEN YOU ADD BAKING SODA TO A HYDROCHLORIC ACID SOLUTION, IT TURNS INTO TABLE SALT, CARBON DIOXIDE, AND WATER. THAT'S HOW ANTACID WORKS FOR AN UPSET STOMACH.
WATER MAIN

SOLUTION—A LIQUID IN WHICH SOMETHING HAS BEEN DISSOLVED

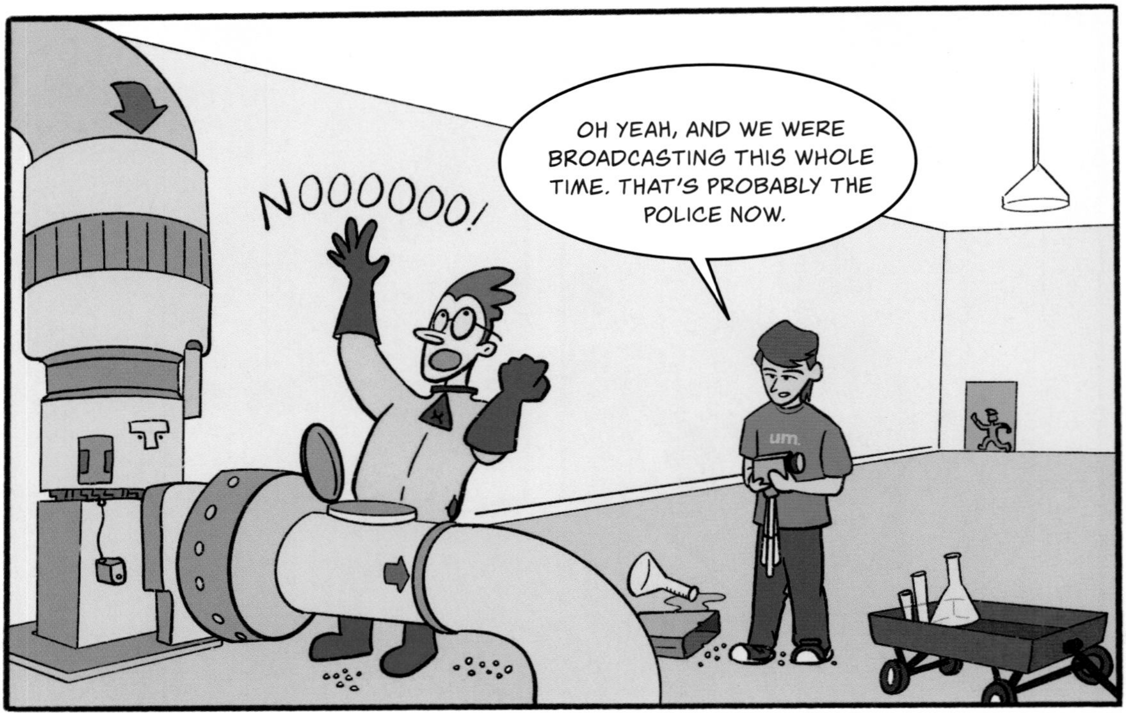
NOOOOOO!
OH YEAH, AND WE WERE BROADCASTING THIS WHOLE TIME. THAT'S PROBABLY THE POLICE NOW.

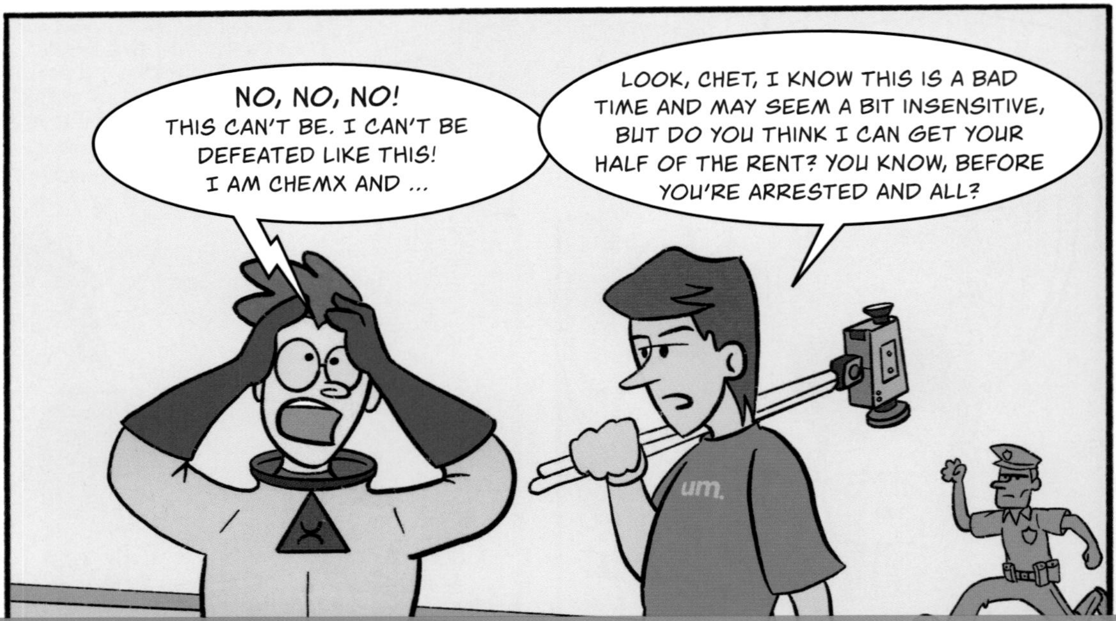
NO, NO, NO! THIS CAN'T BE. I CAN'T BE DEFEATED LIKE THIS! I AM CHEMX AND ...
LOOK, CHET, I KNOW THIS IS A BAD TIME AND MAY SEEM A BIT INSENSITIVE, BUT DO YOU THINK I CAN GET YOUR HALF OF THE RENT? YOU KNOW, BEFORE YOU'RE ARRESTED AND ALL?

Most plastics do not react with acids. This is true for glass too. This is why acids are commonly stored in plastic or glass containers. But the opposite is true with acids and metals. Acids react with most metals and cause the metal to rust or dissolve.

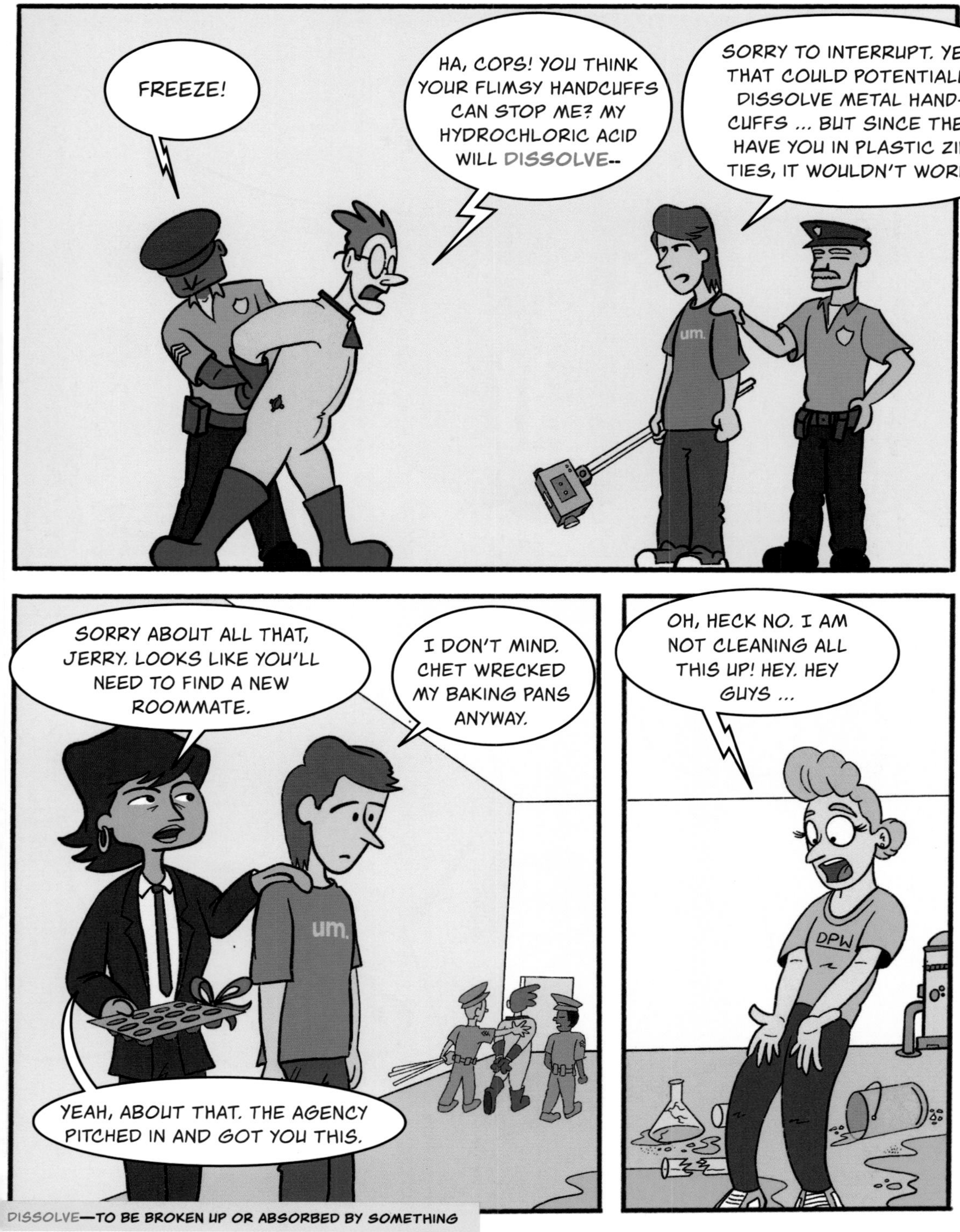
FREEZE!
HA, COPS! YOU THINK YOUR FLIMSY HANDCUFFS CAN STOP ME? MY HYDROCHLORIC ACID WILL DISSOLVE--
SORRY TO INTERRUPT. YES, THAT COULD POTENTIALLY DISSOLVE METAL HAND-CUFFS ... BUT SINCE THEY HAVE YOU IN PLASTIC ZIP TIES, IT WOULDN'T WORK.
um.
SORRY ABOUT ALL THAT, JERRY. LOOKS LIKE YOU'LL NEED TO FIND A NEW ROOMMATE.
I DON'T MIND. CHET WRECKED MY BAKING PANS ANYWAY.
um.
YEAH, ABOUT THAT. THE AGENCY PITCHED IN AND GOT YOU THIS.
OH, HECK NO. I AM NOT CLEANING ALL THIS UP! HEY. HEY GUYS ...
DPW

DISSOLVE—TO BE BROKEN UP OR ABSORBED BY SOMETHING

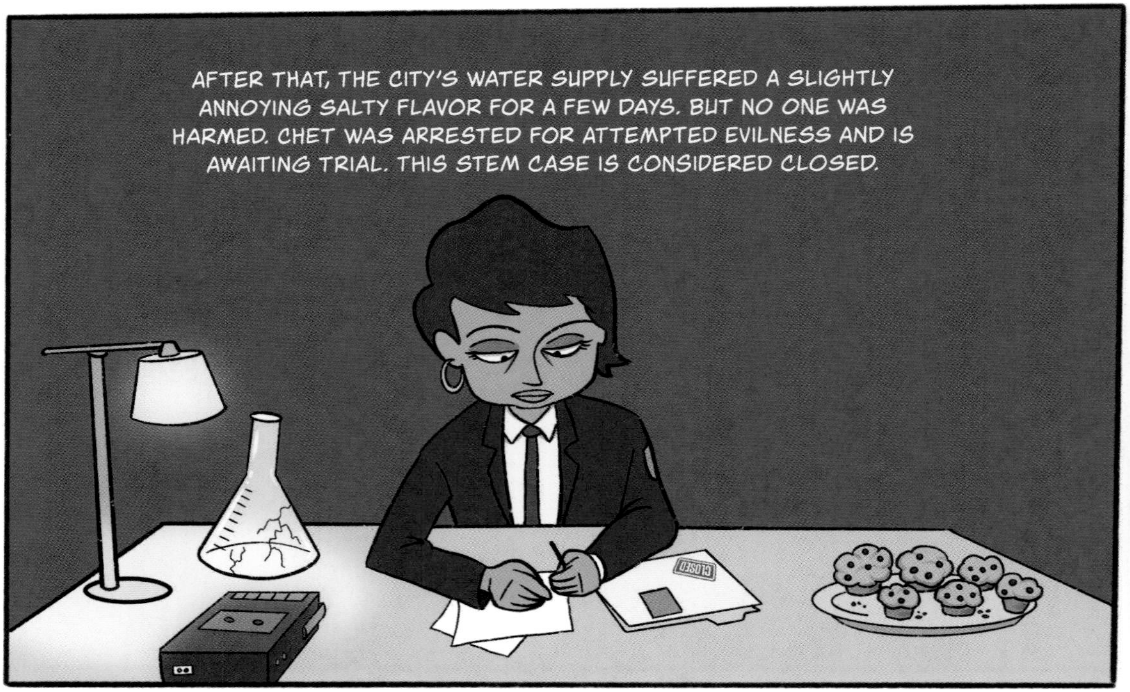
AFTER THAT, THE CITY'S WATER SUPPLY SUFFERED A SLIGHTLY ANNOYING SALTY FLAVOR FOR A FEW DAYS. BUT NO ONE WAS HARMED. CHET WAS ARRESTED FOR ATTEMPTED EVILNESS AND IS AWAITING TRIAL. THIS STEM CASE IS CONSIDERED CLOSED.

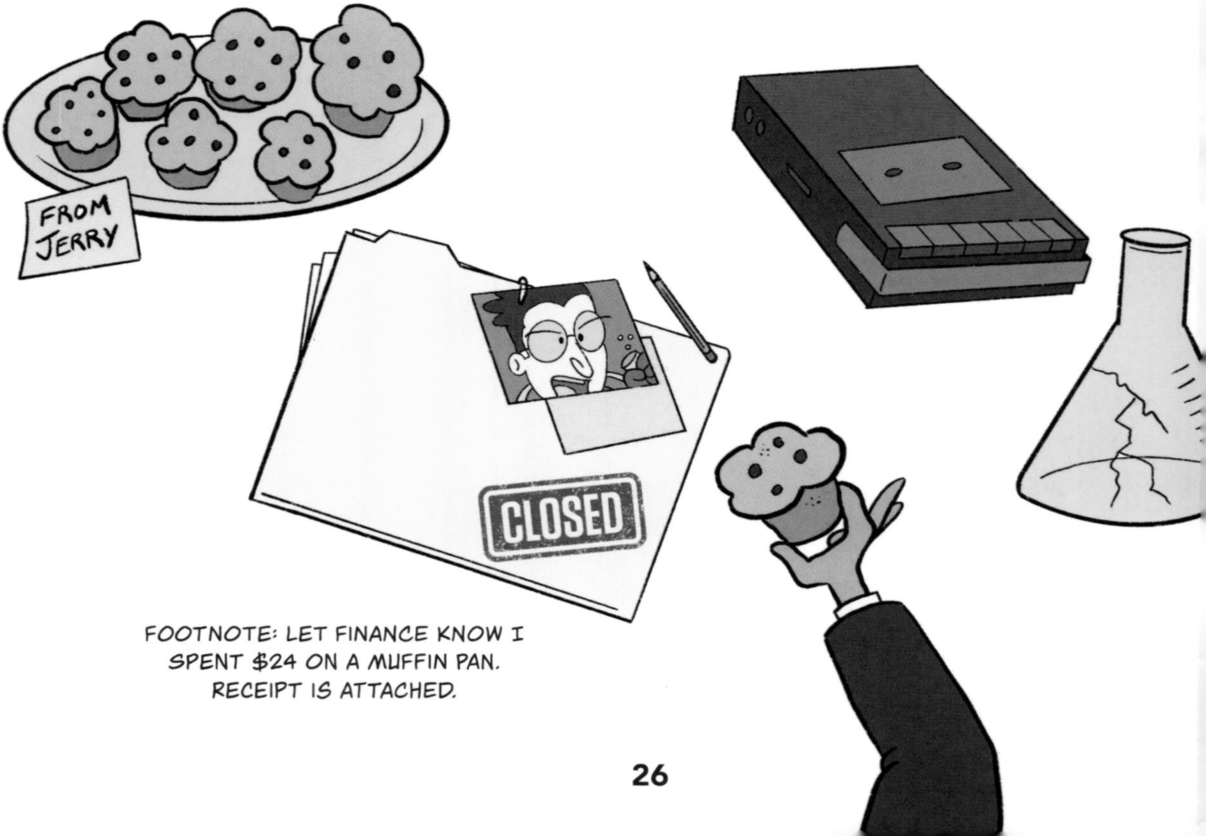
FROM JERRY
CLOSED
FOOTNOTE: LET FINANCE KNOW I SPENT $24 ON A MUFFIN PAN. RECEIPT IS ATTACHED.

Acids and Metals

Acids react with most metals, usually dissolving or destroying the metal over time. This is known as acid corrosion. Unlike acid and base reactions that form water, acids react with metals to generate a salt and gas. Acids can react with metals in different ways to reduce, or oxidize, the metal. These types of reactions are called electrochemical reactions. For example, when hydrochloric acid (HCl) reacts with zinc (Zn), the zinc metal can replace the hydrogen ion (H+). This forms hydrogen gas (H2) and a salt called zinc chloride (ZnCl2). This is also true for common metals like stainless steel. HCl reacts with stainless steel, causing the metal to corrode and generating a salt and gas.

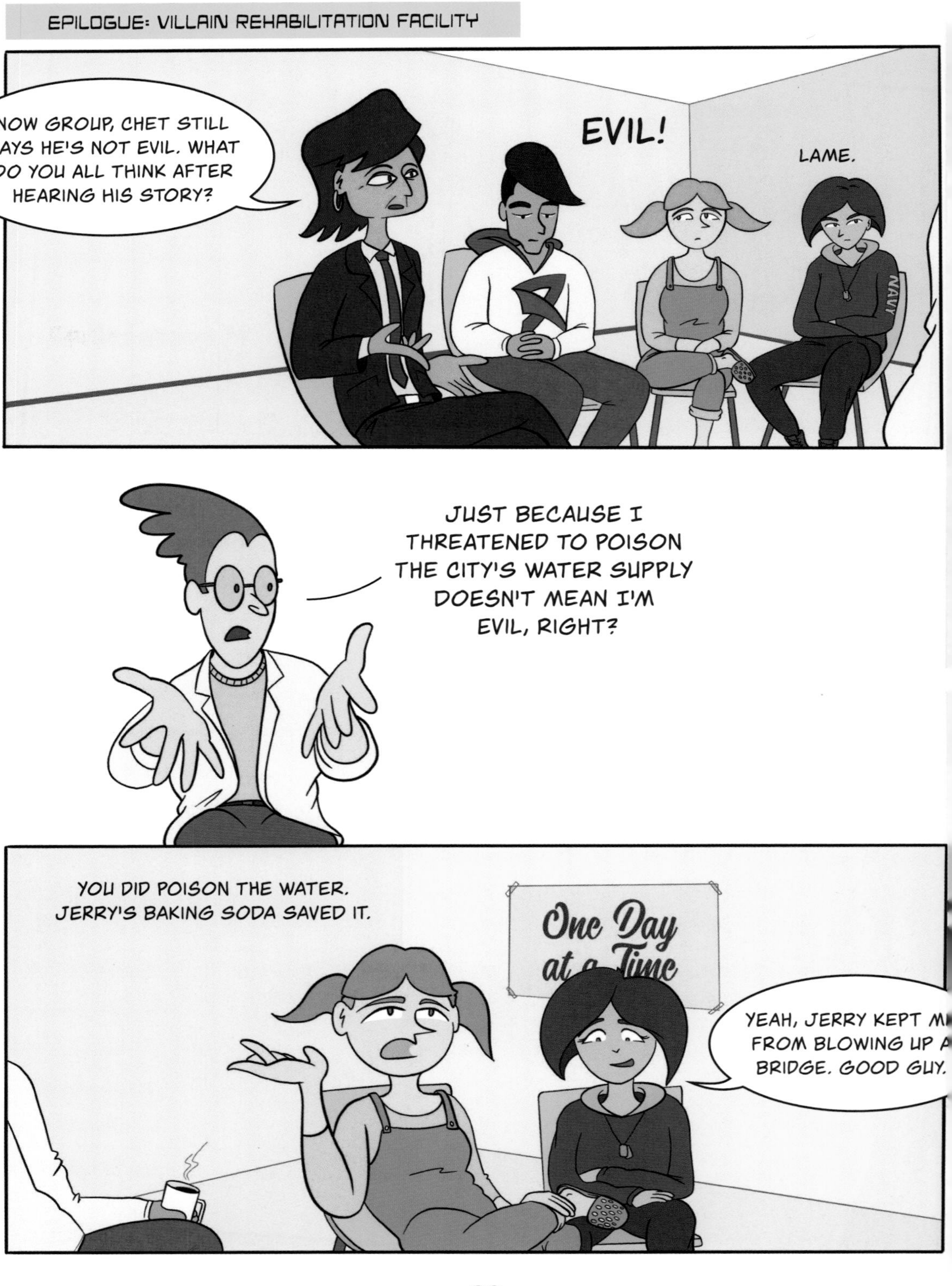
EPILOGUE: VILLAIN REHABILITATION FACILITY
NOW GROUP, CHET STILL SAYS HE'S NOT EVIL. WHAT DO YOU ALL THINK AFTER HEARING HIS STORY?
EVIL!
LAME.
NAVY
JUST BECAUSE I THREATENED TO POISON THE CITY'S WATER SUPPLY DOESN'T MEAN I'M EVIL, RIGHT?
YOU DID POISON THE WATER. JERRY'S BAKING SODA SAVED IT.
One Day at a Time
YEAH, JERRY KEPT M FROM BLOWING UP A BRIDGE. GOOD GUY.

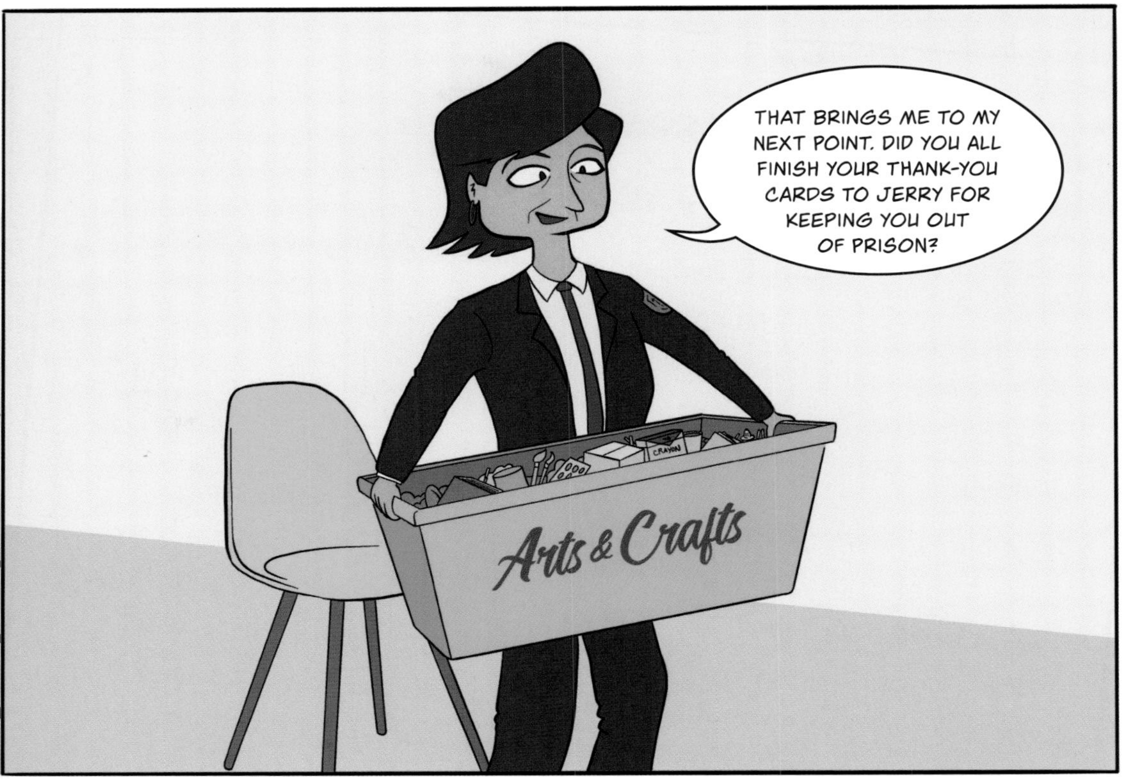
THAT BRINGS ME TO MY NEXT POINT. DID YOU ALL FINISH YOUR THANK-YOU CARDS TO JERRY FOR KEEPING YOU OUT OF PRISON?
Arts & Crafts
CRAYON

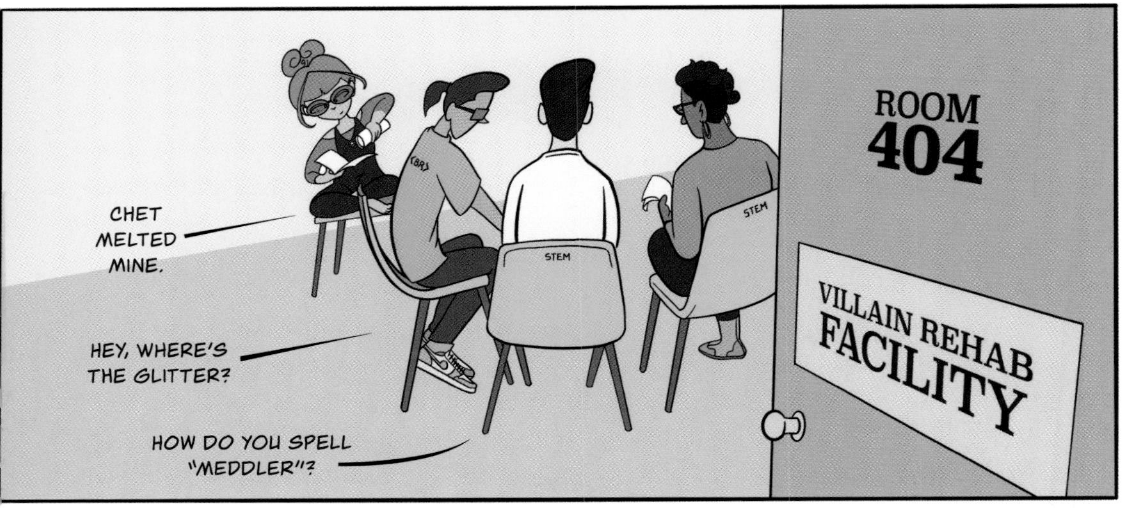
ROOM 404
VILLAIN REHAB FACILITY
CHET MELTED MINE.
HEY, WHERE'S THE GLITTER?
HOW DO YOU SPELL "MEDDLER"?
STEM
STEM

Acids and Bases—
They're Everywhere!

Acid and base reactions happen all around us during every second of the day. These acidic and basic chemicals can be found in our houses and in the food we eat! You may have heard the phrase "pH balanced" or "pH level." pH is used to measure how acidic or basic something is.

Common cleaning products can be acidic or basic depending on what is being cleaned. For instance, if you needed to clean a dirty toilet bowl or remove rust stains, you'd want to use a product with a low pH level (acidic). But if your parents asked you to wash those greasy dishes that have been piling up, you'd want to use a product with a high pH (alkaline) to help separate and break down the fats and oils.

We find acidic and alkaline chemicals in nature too. Orange juice, lemons, and tomatoes are all slightly acidic. Foods like broccoli, celery, and beets are alkaline. To help break down these foods, we have gastric acid in our stomachs. This important digestive fluid is a mixture of hydrochloric acid (HCl) and salts like potassium chloride (KCl) and sodium chloride ($NaCl$). Gastric acid has a pH of 2. This means it is very acidic, which is very important for our stomachs to digest the food we eat—like blueberry muffins!